FPL
747
65 16 $35.00

W9-BYH-174

NOV 06 2003

FRAMINGHAM PUBLIC LIBRARY
NOV 06 2003

innovative
interiors

innovative interiors

Vinny Lee

interiors

Watson-Guptill Publications / New York

Dedication
To AWJ and all my office staff for their moral support.

First published in the United States in 2003 by
Watson-Guptill Publications
a division of VNU Business Media, Inc.
770 Broadway, New York, New York 10003
www.watsonguptill.com

First published in Great Britain in 2002 by
Pavilion
A member of **Chrysalis** Books plc
in association with Times Newspapers Ltd
THE TIMES

Text © Vinny Lee 2002
Design and layout © Pavilion Books Ltd.
Designed by Helen Lewis
Picture research by Jess Walton

The moral right of the author and illustrator has been asserted.

All rights reserved. No part of this publication may be reproduced or used in any form or by any means—graphic, electronic, or mechanical, including photocopying, recording, or information storage-and-retrieval systems—without the prior permission of the publisher.

Library of Congress Control Number: 2002108834

ISBN: 0-8230-2517-9

Manufactured in Singapore

1 2 3 4 5 6 / 07 06 05 04 03 02

JACKET IMAGES:
FRONT: The weekend Hamptons home of Todd Hase, furnished with a mix of old and contemporary furniture placed in a pale setting.
BACK: Kristina Borjesson's open-plan living area in the South Bank area of the River Thames in London, overlooking the Tate Modern art gallery and the Millenium Bridge.

PREVIOUS PAGES:
LEFT: A Tom Dixon spiral light in the corner of Stephanie Churchill's first-floor bedroom.
RIGHT: The oversized sofa in the sitting area of Dominic Richards's apartment, with the slit opening looking through to the kitchen behind.

contents

Introduction

RIGHT: The first-floor living space of Peter Ting's house, with colourful inset panels painted by Brian Kennedy on the wall of built-in cupboards.

Decorating a home involves various important structural elements, such as the division of space, access to daylight and priority of function. But once these basics are taken care of, you can turn your attention to customizing the rooms, adding character and colour. It is the combination of all these things that make a truly personal and individual home.

Although you will have your own ideas and may already have chosen furniture or a colour scheme for a particular room, it is always useful to see how other people, especially talented and creative designers with innovative ideas, have approached a similar space. The inventive features in other peoples' homes are often inspirational when it comes to arranging and decorating our own houses and apartments. By looking into the decoration and lifestyles of others we can identify solutions to problems we may be facing and see how designers, architects and other imaginative people have solved them.

In the wide variety of locations shown in this book – from newly built family homes to twelfth-century churches, and from converted warehouses to rooftop apartments – we see how people have interpreted trends and styles to suit their tastes, or chosen to totally ignore them and go their own way. These days interior style isn't so much about following rules slavishly; it is concerned with creating an environment that provides a home, a place where you feel secure, comfortable and relaxed.

Each of the residences chosen for **Innovative Interiors** has been individually created to provide for the necessities of life as well as for indulgences, and you can tell a lot about a person by how these aspects are catered for. Public rooms such as sitting and dining areas are often showcases for prized possessions or collections. They are spaces where friends, family and strangers are entertained, so they tend to be more restrained and

ABOVE LEFT: Contemporary furniture by Garouste & Bonette in the dining room of Stephanie Churchill's London home.

ABOVE RIGHT: The mezzanine landing of Mark Budden's converted ink factory apartment.

in some cases less personal. The most intimate and private of rooms is the bedroom, and this is often where a decoration whim or fantasy is indulged.

The inner, more personal secrets of the home are increasingly of interest, as are the psychological links and relationships between people and their environment. In our surroundings at work there is often a certain pressure to conform or to subdue one's personality, but within the home, one's personal space, an individual's identity can truly be expressed or revealed.

Amongst the houses and apartments shown here are some that illustrate examples of this phenomenon. The outwardly flamboyant and colourful Brazilian fashion designer Carlos Miele, whose decorative and sexy clothes are favoured by actresses and film stars, lives in a minimal, almost austere rooftop apartment in São Paulo. On the other hand, the reserved and reclusive designer Emanuel Ungaro has a richly decorated and ornately colourful interior in his restored historic home in the south of France.

New York fashion designer Betsey Johnson is known for her flamboyant and colourful clothes, and her home conspicuously reflects those aspects of her character and style. Yet Italian textile executive Anna Zegna has made a home that caters for two sides of her character. Part of her house is a traditional home on two floors, but on the third she has made a contrasting modern, serene interior where she feels fresh and free from the constraints of a busy working and family life.

For a few people, designing, building and furnishing their home can be a catalyst, even a life-changing experience. On the outskirts of Sydney, Ken Israel found that creating his ecologically inspired home was a cathartic and restorative experience. After years of working in a high-speed executive job in the city, he found constructing and living in his forest home gave him a new perspective and lease on life. For many people, their home is a haven of peace, a refuge from their busy working lives. As fashion designer Anna Valentine says, 'Simplicity creates calm.'

Innovative Interiors not only offers the opportunity to be inspired by the homes of others. It also provides a unique guide to various styles and types of building, and to lifestyles from around the world. When you are creating your own space you can take elements from any of these locations and combine them to make your own individual and innovative interior.

classic

In the late 1990s Joseph, his wife Isabel and their daughter Gigi moved to a three-storey house in a residential Chelsea street, not far from his flagship London store. From the outside the building was Arts and Crafts with a half-timbered exterior and diamond-pane leaded windows, but inside they created a modern home. The scheme focuses on quality and simplicity, and incorporates natural materials such as wood and stone, which became an important part of the overall design. 'It was time to move on to a cleaner, less indulgent style', he says.

In the process of converting the house the Ettedguis created three apartments under one roof. The first apartment is the public space, on the ground floor. Here there were a number of small rooms but these were knocked through to create a more open-plan scheme. This not only made it an easier and more practical place in which to entertain friends, but also, by opening up this lower level, it helped to make it lighter, allowing the daylight from windows at the front and back of the house to reach the inner areas.

With the help of French designer Christian Liaigre, who had designed Joseph's offices on Boulevard Raspail in Paris, they furnished this large room with unfussy but beautifully made pieces in dark wenge wood. This contemporary furniture provides a dramatic contrast to the setting of plain, almost stark white walls and unpretentious polished wood floors. Much of the furniture was specially created by Liaigre and tailored to fit in and around specific areas.

The ground-floor 'public' areas were designed for entertaining and sitting with friends, and Joseph describes it as being 'like a hotel lobby'. The seating is arranged so that there are several small, more intimate groups rather than a single large one. Along the main wall, just inside the entrance

tailor-made

Joseph Ettedgui, one of London's legendary retailers and style aficionados, created his shops with leading architects and designers, who in turn influenced the decor of his home. Furnished with a mix of classic and contemporary furniture, his house has a simple, understated scheme of white walls with polished floors in the public spaces and carpet in the private rooms for a softer and more informal feel.

PREVIOUS PAGES: The daybed in James and Deirdre Dyson's sitting room, with a view through the arch to the dining room.

LEFT: A dark wood-panelled archway leads to the living room. In the dining room, candle holders by André Dubreuil rest on the polished table, while a 'billiard-table' style lamp hangs overhead. On the end wall is a pastel drawing by the sculptor Bernar Venet.

ABOVE: The side panel of the simple staircase leading to the first floor provides a backdrop for a sculptural pillar candlestick by the Parisian designer Anne Severine. Also seen here is the richly coloured wood flooring that runs throughout the ground floor.

hall, is a red custom-made upholstered sofa, above which is a black-and-white picture of Celia Birtwell by David Hockney. Another Hockney drawing hangs on one of the dining room walls.

Opposite the red sofa, forming the second area of seating, are two dark-brown leather chairs and two more sofas. This time the leather is dark brown and the upholstery is in a light but compatible golden hessian. A long leather cushion gives extra comfort and padding to the third area, a window seat, which is built in below the diamond-paned bow window.

Beyond the 'lobby' there is an archway, with dark wood-panelled facings, leading to the dining room. Here one wall is dominated by a large abstract pastel drawing by the sculptor Bernar Venet, and the centre of the room is occupied by a long table over which hangs an oblong cream shade, which Joseph describes as being like a billiard-table light.

A new, angular wooden staircase leads from the end of the dining room to the silver-grey carpeted first floor and Joseph and Isabel's private apartment. Directly in front of the staircase is a small sitting room decorated in warm, relaxing shades of oatmeal and honey. The furniture consists of two classic 1950s Scandinavian chairs with pale wood arms, a sofa with rounded form, a low coffee table, and a leather desk and stool from the French atelier of Hermès.

A collection of Lalique vases, one of Joseph's favoured collectibles, are arranged on the windowsill where the light catches the relief patterns on the surface. On the stone mantel of the fireplace is a figure of a jazz-style guitar player bought over twenty years ago from a flea market in Paris.

To the left of the sitting room is the simply furnished bedroom with an en suite bathroom. Looking around this sparingly decorated room, Joseph explains part of his design philosophy. 'It is easier to have little,' he says. 'I think you have to be clever to mix things well. It can be difficult to get the right combination of diverse types of design.'

The third apartment, on the top floor of the house, is Gigi's, with her colourful bedroom, bathroom and playroom. This space is full of life and vitality, and a contrast to the formality and carefully crafted scheme of the main living spaces on the ground floor of this family home.

Joseph's interest in fashion and clothes spilt over into interior design when he set about creating a style for his shops. In turn the architecture of the shops and the designers he met affected the way he approached his personal space at home, and also led him to develop an interiors and furniture section within the shops. The creative circle is now complete, but even Joseph admits he never stops learning.

RIGHT: On the first floor the private sitting room is furnished with 1950s Scandinavian armchairs and a Hermès leather desk and stool. Objets d'art include a couple of Joseph's collection of Lalique vases, which catch the light from the window and, on the mantel above the fireplace, a jazz-player sculpture.

FOLLOWING PAGES: The custom-built sofa, of wenge wood with red upholstery, is a focal point in the lobby-style sitting area on the ground floor. The sofa is set beneath a picture of Celia Birtwell by David Hockney.

LEFT: The sunny first floor family sitting room with its restored shutters at the long windows is one of the places where the delicate period panelling and architrave can be seen. The marble fire-surround was retrieved from under layers of old paint.

RIGHT: The airy ground floor dining room, with original Queen Anne features, is decorated in soft colours and with pieces of Deirdre's work, such as the still-life painting that hangs over the fireplace and the rug beneath the table.

classic update

James and Deirdre Dyson have restored a period home in London using their diverse talents. James is the inventor of modern domestic appliances such as the cyclonic vacuum cleaner, and his artist wife Deirdre is a talented painter who also runs a contemporary rug company. Together they have created a series of elegant and refined rooms with classic references, using soft colours to bring warmth and tranquillity.

ABOVE: Contemporary design, featuring metal and glass, is found in the practical basement kitchen, which, like the rest of the house, adheres to the Dyson dictum of simple but strong lines and uncluttered spaces.

LEFT: On the first floor at the back of the house, the master bedroom is furnished with carefully selected pieces of timeless furniture, which complement the modern carpet and bed throw. The en suite bathroom, glimpsed here through the open door, has a classic roll-top bath.

James and Deirdre Dyson spent over a year restoring their Chelsea home, a Queen Anne house built around 1705. They invested much time in researching the history of the building, as well as the style appropriate to that period, so that they could restore and decorate it sympathetically.

The house is simply decorated and carefully but sparingly furnished. There are panelled shutters at most windows, and the walls are painted with matt-finish pale colours, with the panel architraves picked out in a slightly darker shade. The original staircase, which, because of its age and settlement, leans slightly, still has the original barley-sugar twist banisters supporting the mellow and well-worn wooden handrail. The relatively unadorned, almost flush marble surrounds to the fireplaces were uncovered from beneath layers of paint, and the warping of the wooden wall panelling was repaired by expert craftsmen.

On the ground floor, to the front of the house, there is a formal dining room with a round table, chairs and two small side tables. Concealed behind a panelled cupboard to the right of the fireplace are a sink, refrigerator and bar area. One of Deirdre's paintings hangs over the fireplace, and one of her rugs echoes the colours in the painting.

Beyond the dining room, through an archway, is a sitting room with a daybed and an armchair, and in a small recess off this main room is a study area with an antique wooden desk and a chair. The long windows of these rear rooms overlook the enclosed garden with its long, Zen-like pool.

The ancient stairs make their way up past a half landing and cloakroom and turn again towards the front of the house until they reach a landing outside the main bedroom on the first floor. This room is to the back of the house and a similar size to the sitting room below, with an en suite bathroom over the small study. For privacy this bedroom has fine voile curtains. A coloured shot-silk throw complements the rug.

At this level, to the front of the house, is the wide, sunny family sitting room with long shuttered windows and cream upholstered sofas facing each other on either side of the hearth and marble fire surround. A selection of modern floor-standing lights at either end of the sofas brings an element of contemporary style into this otherwise classic setting.

As the wooden stairs rise to the top floor the panelling becomes noticeably more simple, and as you arrive on the last landing you enter what used to be the servants' quarters. The smallest room, reached by six further steps, is about the size of a double-door cupboard and was, Deirdre has been told, the boot boy's room. At this level there are two more bedrooms and a bathroom. The classic roll-top bath has been placed on a lead tray to protect the ancient original floorboards and the ceiling of the room below.

For a family known to be at the cutting edge of contemporary design, this curiously calm period home shows few signs of modern living—that is, until you go down to the basement. Here you walk into a kitchen with steel-clad units and reinforced-glass splashbacks. It feels as though you have stepped into not only a different house, but also another era.

In common with the rest of the house, the kitchen scheme is clean and uncluttered, but it is more hard-edged and plainly practical. A round informal dining table offers some respite against the angular lines, and various pieces of Deirdre's artwork add an element of colour.

'At first we didn't hang any paintings on the walls,' says Deirdre, 'but we found that a little too austere. The ones we subsequently put up had to be chosen carefully to fit within the borders of the panelling or so that they would hang evenly over them. Painting can be a solitary occupation. What I enjoy is being involved in two worlds, one that revolves around painting and the other with the carpet business and the buzz of London life.' In the interior decoration of her period home she has brought together the creations that result from these two different aspects of her life.

prime location

Garden designer and film-set decorator Ann Mollo and her partner, production designer Jon Bunker, live in an unusual home in west London made up of two neighbouring houses linked on certain floors. The style and decor have been strongly influenced by their work in films. The house features theatrical paint techniques and recycled props as well as real and make-believe antiques.

Ann's home, on the edge of a picturesque, predominantly Georgian square, consists of two houses that have at various times been joined, separated and re-joined. They consist of a number of small rooms, a few of which have been opened up to create slightly larger spaces, each decorated with its own distinctive scheme.

The top storey of the house spreads between the two buildings and has a strongly Gothic influence to its decoration. The 'snug' room (in the second house) has a TV console made out of an old font cover from a demolished church and bought from an antiques shop, set on a base with folding doors. A tapestry panel on a tall stand that rests beside the fireplace was once used by Victorian gentlewomen to prevent the heat from colouring their complexions, and two small gilded sconce brackets support pieces of porcelain on the painted chimney breast.

Contacts for finding the font cover and many other unusual artefacts are a direct result of the couple's extensive

LEFT: On the side wall, over the desk in the sitting room on the upper level of the first house, is a portrait of Ann and one of her dogs, painted in this same setting. Some pieces from Ann's creamware collection rest on the coffee table, and antique baldaquins frame the windows.

ABOVE: The-blue panelled and painted bathroom, with its Gothic-style peg rail, looks through to the dressing room beyond on the top floor of the first house.

CENTRE: The 'snug' TV room is furnished with a cabinet made from a font lid and a second-hand Gothic-style door that leads to the dressing room.

work researching and propping for films such as *The French Lieutenant's Woman*, for which Ann received an Oscar nomination for her work. Yet in this house all the pieces come together to create a highly original and unusual eclectic style.

From the 'snug' room an unglazed door, bought second-hand from another antiques dealer, leads to the walk-in dressing room with two walls of wardrobes fitted with Gothic arched doors, some with mirror insets. Unlike many of the other doors, these are not antiques but were constructed by Jon; even so they do have something of the flavour of a Dracula movie set about them. By the window is a gentleman's antique dressing stand with a low circular shelf for cufflinks and shirt studs and a raised mirror on a stand, beside which is a holder for a candle.

Next door in the bathroom a peg rail is again Jon's handiwork. These three rooms are painted in white with a soft, muted grey-blue. This particular shade of blue is a colour the couple made up themselves by mixing various shades until the right one was achieved.

The bedroom, also on this top floor, is Oriental in style, with decorative bamboo picture rails and mirror surrounds made to match the couple's collection of faux-bamboo furniture. Jon made a cast of a section of bamboo and created metres of it with plaster, which were later painted and then glued to the walls. Pieces of antique fabric and tapestry, many the remains of dressings used on sets, have been made into cushions, and the curtains are draped dramatically with generous silk tassels.

On the floor below, in the second house, is a Gothic-style library stacked with books. Beside this, to the back of the house with a view of the garden, is the creamware room where a major part of Ann's collection of china creamware is displayed in a simple glass-fronted cabinet.

A secret door, hung with framed paintings to look as though it is really a part of the wall, links these two 'next door' rooms to the first house. In the first house at this level is the sitting room, once two smaller rooms but now opened into one. A black-and-gilt sofa sits under an ornate gilt-framed mirror and between two tall windows framed with antique fabric baldaquins. The room is richly furnished and decorated and comes into its own in the evening when the artificial light sparkles on the many gilt, silver and glass items.

The staircase that links the floors of the main house is painted with faux-green panelling below the dado and a soft mottled peach colour above, a task finely executed by a film scenic artist friend. On the ground floor, off the narrow entrance hall, is Ann's book-lined study. Jon's is in the second house and reached by a separate front door. Ann's room has a large door, originally from a private club and once used in a film. Its sizeable glass panels enable her to sit at her desk and gaze through the dining area to the conservatory and her beloved garden. At the back of the conservatory, reached through double doors, is the compact galley-style kitchen.

Ann and Jon have employed many of the tricks of their trade to make this house a prime location, an unusual mix of Gothic and chinoiserie styles dressed with movie props.

ABOVE: A corner of the main bedroom shows part of the fake bamboo rails and frames that were made in plaster and painted to match the faux-bamboo furniture.

LEFT: The white bathroom situated on the first floor at the back of the house has a well-upholstered easy chair in which to relax and unwind. Shelves of deep pile towels add to the sense of luxury.

RIGHT: The first floor sitting room at the front of the house contains many items of contemporary artwork, including a sculpted head by Oriel Harwood on the mantel above the fireplace.

moving with the times

Dutch-born Stephanie Churchill's south London house has evolved with her changing lifestyle, from a busy family home to a live-and-work space, and finally into a spacious residence for one. The decor has also changed, becoming more simple and focused, furnishing a setting in which her growing collection of work by contemporary artists and craftspeople can be displayed.

Stephanie Churchill's terraced house has changed over the years from a bustling family home to her own individual sanctuary. Milestones have included her three children growing up and leaving, the public relations company she founded in the basement developing so successfully that it had to move to larger premises, and also her divorce. As her life has altered, so has the house. All the rooms have had different functions. The dining room was once a study, the room that is now the study has at various times been the kitchen, a nursery, the dog room and a bicycle storage area. The dressing room was also, at one stage, a nursery; and where the PR offices were in the basement there is now a private cinema.

The rooms have also undergone style changes. Ten years ago the house was full of colour, paintings, cushions, carpets and wall hangings, but with the end of that particular era came a purge, which resulted in vanloads of furniture and pictures being sent off to auctions and sales. This editing down of possessions has left more space and the opportunity for Stephanie to tailor the decoration to suit herself.

Now everything in the house has been selected for a reason, rather than bought to suit another's needs. With this cleansing and reorganizing Stephanie found that she became more selective about what she bought because she was focused on how she wanted her home to look.

Off the long, narrow hallway is the dining room with deep-rust-coloured walls and a decorative stone fireplace. Over the mantel is a row of black-and-white photographs by David Hiscock which stand out dramatically against the richly coloured walls. From the centre of the ceiling an old Dutch chandelier hangs over the table. The tall windows which look out towards a leafy park are simply framed with lengths of plain white linen. These are easy to launder, so they keep their pristine appearance.

Although a colourful and inviting space, the dining room is not often used because the round table in the adjacent kitchen is where friends most often choose to dine. The kitchen table, made from the old joists of Unilever House, is the only thing that has stayed in the same position.

At the back of the hallway on this level there is a small room, currently the study, where reference material, computers and telephones are kept. Stairs lead down from here to the basement laundry room, a guest bedroom, conservatory and the cinema. The cinema is a naturally dark room because it is below street level, and has been furnished with deep, comfortable sofas and a large upholstered ottoman to make the experience of home viewing, on the large retractable screen, an indulgent and enjoyable pastime.

LEFT: The richly coloured ground-floor kitchen also doubles as a dining place with a circular wooden table where friends congregate. The old fireplace is now a useful storage area containing two deep baskets.

To the rear of the house on the first floor there is a white-painted bathroom. This has also been tailored to make it a restful and relaxing room, with shelves stacked with thick towels and small, purple velvet bags of scented soap. A large comfortable armchair provides a place for unwinding and recuperating after a bath or simply for sitting and watching the clouds pass by.

Beyond the bathroom on the first floor landing there is another door on the left which opens into the main bedroom. This is a calm beige-and-white space with a large fireplace, beside which is a huge, glittering amethyst geode. In the other corner is a large golden spiral light by Tom Dixon which casts swirling circular shadows on the ceiling when lit. The sizeable bed is dressed with crisp white linen sheets, soft woollen blankets and a fur throw.

Beyond the bedroom, at the front of the house, is the sitting room with a row of three tall windows overlooking the green expanse of Battersea Park. These tall windows and the elevated position of this room mean that it is bright and light even on overcast days.

One wall of the sitting room is taken up by an old Dutch dresser inherited from Stephanie's grandparents. The doors of the dresser are permanently open, displaying the shelves inside which are filled with framed photographs and pieces of contemporary art and craft work. On the mantel of the fireplace on the opposite wall is a plaster head by sculptor Oriel Harwood.

On the top floor, in what was originally one of her children's bedrooms, Stephanie now has her own well-ordered and arranged dressing room. The walls are lined with open hanging space and shelves which enable her to select clothes and change, or to pack and be ready to go at a moment's notice.

This house has a mix of colourful, plain and dark spaces, each designed to be comfortable and relaxing, and each by its decor creating a different mood or environment in which to unwind. It is a tranquil home that has been decorated with care, not minimally, but with carefully chosen pieces that have meaning or memories.

RIGHT: Work surfaces in the kitchen have been designed to bring colour to the space. Iroko wood and gunmetal paint contrast with the white and glass splashbacks. An overhead lightwell brings additional natural light to this basement area of the house.

FAR RIGHT: The view into Henry's study with its hand-painted frottage-effect wall and antique artwork. To the right, the gilded panel with display niches is surrounded by glass insets which allow daylight from the hallway to come in and the view of the sculptural staircase to be admired.

ahead of the curve

Film and documentary maker Henry Dent-Brocklehurst's family home is Sudeley, a fifteenth-century castle in Gloucestershire, but his own home with his wife, model Lili Maltese, is in a west London house which they have extensively remodelled to bring in light and a feeling of space. This five-level house has also been designed to accommodate historic pieces of artwork and contemporary furniture.

Soon after he purchased the house, Henry Dent-Brocklehurst discovered that it was infested with dry rot. The interior had to be completely gutted, a huge undertaking, but one that gave him the opportunity to tailor the space to suit himself and his wife Lili.

To reconstruct the inside, Henry called in a team of architects whose work with glass and the manipulation of light he admired. Inside the shell of four exterior walls they devised a scheme centred around a new, dramatic, angular staircase, each piece of which had to be specially made and wrangled into place because the layout of the house is off centre.

The attic was also opened up to provide a fifth level, and the staircase to it now crosses over the main staircase, creating a drawbridge-like feature. Light from a large skylight in the roof pours down through the open sides of the stairs and penetrates the basement kitchen/living area through glass panels. The glass panels are set into sections of the wooden flooring at each level, and one is also disconcertingly placed immediately inside the front door. On entering, it momentarily appears as though there is nothing beneath your feet.

When the basic structural and architectural work was finished, the house had five levels. In the basement there was a large open-plan kitchen, relaxing and dining area with a wall of glass doors opening onto a garden. On the ground floor there was the entrance hall with the dramatic central staircase, Henry's study and an evening sitting room. Above, the first floor accommodated the master bedroom with en suite bathroom, followed on the second floor by Lili's study and a spare bedroom and bathroom. Finally at the fifth level there were two more spare bedrooms and a bathroom.

To help bring a sense of homeliness to their house the Dent-Brocklehursts asked specialist painter and designer Nick Esch and landscape designer Sarah Howard for ideas. It was also Esch's task to bring together the diverse elements and make them work in harmony. This included finding the right places for a number of artworks and antiques that had been brought from Sudeley, including an ebony-and-gilt clock and some old prints and paintings that didn't seem to sit comfortably anywhere in the contemporary interior. Lili, who is from Hawaii, wanted colour in the house.

In the kitchen, colour was introduced into the work surfaces; the tops were finished with warm Iroko wood and MDF (medium-density fiberboard) units sprayed with a gunmetal surface and edged with a copper lip on the bottom return. The adjacent dining area is dominated by a long solid elm table made by designer John Edmonds.

In the lounging area there are two camel coloured sofas scattered with cashmere throws and cushions. Opposite the

sofas is a simple limestone fire surround with a raised hearth deep enough to perch on. Through the glass doors at the back of the sitting area is the excavated garden with stepped banks and built-in seats around a blue limestone table.

Upstairs in the study and more formal sitting room the walls were hand-painted with a frottage effect of muted gold over a red background, which creates an intimate and opulent feel in artificial light and makes a perfect backdrop to the antique clock and paintings. The study has a desk and filing system covered in a rich red leather by Bill Amberg.

Dividing the hall and evening sitting room there is a gilded panel with niches for artefacts. The panel is attached to the outer walls and ceiling by clear glass insets that allow additional natural light into the room during the day.

The main bedroom has sea-green shot-silk curtains and similarly coloured voiles at the window. The room is dominated by a large *lit bateau* and two deep wardrobes, which are recessed and disguised in the walls of the archway that leads through to the bathroom. Lili's study on the second floor is painted in a sky blue. The other bedrooms and bathrooms are decorated with white walls and colourful accessories.

'Our home now feels like a suit that has been made to fit', says Lili, as all their requirements for light, space and colour have now been satisfied.

LEFT: The sea-green curtains and voiles at the window of the main bedroom tint the light that comes through them, giving a cool, watery look to the room.

ABOVE: The glass-panel end wall of the open-plan basement folds back to give full access to the excavated garden, which is planted with oleanders and features a blue table.

home sweet home

Cath Kidston runs her own successful fabric and accessory business in London, where she has two shops that mix old ceramics, fabrics and artefacts with her new 'retro' style designs. This mix of old and new has also been the basis of the decoration in the old stone house that is her weekend retreat.

LEFT: The spacious, bright kitchen centres around a pale blue range. Rows of open shelves are neatly stacked with old storage jars collected from junk shops.

ABOVE: In the first of the two sitting rooms there is a deep stone fire-surround, in which the date denoting the origins of the house is carved.

In the Gloucestershire home that Cath and her husband, music producer Hugh Padgham, describe as their 'dream house', they have combined modern and old fabrics with soft period-style prints, traditional pieces of furniture and colourful second-hand accessories to create a style that is comforting and has its roots in the 1950s.

The house is solid and built of stone. The core dates from the late 1600s, with additions to both the sides and back added through the centuries. Cath and Hugh stripped away most of the existing decoration and painted the plastered walls of the house in white and soft off-white shades, giving them a clean background with which to work.

The front door opens into a grand stone-and-wood hallway, but the back door is where most people enter because it leads into the kitchen, which is the bright, light heart of the home and where Cath is most often found. Through this door you pass down a passageway of utility rooms, a larder and a row of hooks where outdoor coats are hung and boots are lined up beneath.

At the end of the passage is the spacious kitchen with a pale blue, enamelled panel stove. A long table covered with a length of old flowery fabric is surrounded by wooden chairs painted bright red. Stools on either side of the stove were a junk shop purchase which were painted red to match the chairs. Open shelves around the sink are neatly stacked with red-and-white storage jars and a bread bin, all of which are vintage rather than new.

From the front of the kitchen a small stone-flagged hall leads to a door which opens to the garden. To the right of this door another one leads to the sitting room. Originally this was one huge room but Cath and Hugh divided it into two smaller, cosier spaces by building a partition of floor-to-ceiling bookcases with a door-sized gap between them.

In the first sitting room there is a large stone fireplace with an ancient date carved into the broad stone lintel of the chimney breast. Against the cool background of stone and cream-painted walls, the red and golden-yellow upholstery coverings on the armchairs is warming and bright. An old quilt is used as a table cover, and rugs also help to make what could feel a chilly room comfortable and inviting. At the foot of the staircase which winds up behind the chimney there is a formal portrait in oils and a dark wood table and antique curved-back chairs.

In the second sitting room a mélange of patterned fabrics, linked again by a theme of red and yellow, gives an almost Provençal feeling to the stone-floored room. A window seat scattered with cushions and rugs provides a viewing point from which to admire the sizeable garden.

The winding stone staircase from the first sitting room goes up to the floor above. The walls of the main bedroom are a soft yellowish-green colour, which complements the delicate, muted purple floral fabric that has been used for curtains and cushion covers. Old woven woollen knee rugs are draped over a well-worn armchair near one of the windows. On a dressing table, another old quilt is employed as a cloth. There is a huge rug on the floor and a hand-crocheted white cotton bedspread. Off the main bedroom is a spacious white bathroom clad with tongue-and-groove panelling. Some of the panels conceal wardrobes, shelves and storage space.

On the other side of the main bedroom is one of the four spare rooms. One is decorated in softest shades of pink and is furnished with an old canopied bed dressed with chintz curtains lined with a rosebud material, part of a collection designed by Cath. The bed is made with a medley of new and old fabrics, including an antique, lace-edged top sheet and a traditional eiderdown. The other guest bedrooms are decorated in a similar style.

Cath's style at home, as in her fabrics, is reassuring because it is reminiscent of places and pictures seen before. It is almost classic with a slightly sentimental edge.

LEFT: Among the four guest bedrooms is this cosy canopied bed, dressed with a mix of Cath's own designs and vintage materials, including an antique lace-edged linen sheet and a feather-filled eiderdown.

ABOVE: The tongue-and-groove panelled walls conceal ample shelf and hanging space. The wood on the walls and floors also insulates the room and makes it cosier.

historical reference

Graham Fraser and Richard Nott were the designers behind the cult fashion label Workers for Freedom, favoured by the Pet Shop Boys, Colin Firth and Joely Richardson. More recently they have become the tenants of an historic National Trust property, Stoneacre in Kent, where they have remodelled part of a wing that was a later addition, and created living quarters which combine a monochromatic scheme with ethnic accessories.

LEFT: The dark brown painted steps and floor of the back staircase lead from the first floor landing and past one of the guest bedrooms before ascending to the attic.

FOLLOWING PAGE, LEFT: On the wood-panelled wall of the private sitting room hangs a steer's skull, a memento of a photographic shoot in Santa Fe. Through the door is the recently refurbished kitchen.

RIGHT: In the immaculate white kitchen with its checkerboard floor there is a mixture of contemporary and traditional styles. The chairs and tables are modern, the cupboards and cabinets traditional country style. A tribal mask adorns the wall.

As guardians of Stoneacre, the house left to the National Trust by Aymer Vallance in 1928, Graham and Richard are responsible for overseeing the care of the gardens and the main hall as well as those rooms that are open to the public.

These rooms include the Great Hall with its huge tie-beams and central hearth in the original fifteenth-century section of the house, the parlour beyond with antique velvet curtains and delicate stained-glass panels in the lead light windows, and the solar or solarium, a room often found in the upper chamber of a medieval house. This room on the first floor has its original fireplace and oriel window.

In the gardens, Graham, now a qualified garden designer, has planted a black border filled with the darkest roses, deep purple cornflowers and midnight poppies. Meanwhile Richard is devoted to the two acres (one hectare) of orchard and wildflower meadow that run across the rear elevation.

Inside the house, behind the 'Private' sign and silk rope that cordons off the north-east wing, they have created a home that is a mix of ancient and modern. The wing, added by Vallance in the 1920s, is constructed from materials salvaged from North Bore Place, a late-sixteenth-century house that was being demolished at nearby Chiddingstone.

The sitting room in this private wing is wood-panelled and has a large stone-framed fireplace set into the wall opposite the window. It is a dark room not only because of the rich panelling but also because the leaded windows are shaded by the large ancient trees in the meadow beyond.

The couple discovered during their first winter in residence that with the history and ambience of the exceptional house came practical dilemmas such as old, draughty windows. But lateral thinking led them to the clever solution of using duvets as curtains. In the sitting room they are concealed behind an outer layer of black taffeta.

The unlikely wall decoration of a steer's head came from a fashion shoot for Workers for Freedom in Sante Fe and the small glass-and-wood table is an original G Plan model found at an antiques market and stripped and stained by Richard. Other furnishings include a wooden African figure from an interior design shop in London, and the lamps are from Liberty in Regent Street.

Beyond the dark sitting room is the kitchen. This room was deep yellow and brown but is now painted white with black-and-white checkerboard linoleum flooring, which has given the room a lighter, brighter appearance. Another piece of Richard's recent restoration handiwork is the linen chest with its new fine mesh panels which, along with the blue Aga

LEFT: The main bedroom has a low, beamed ceiling and timbered walls. The duvet curtains at the windows keep winter draughts at bay. The chairs and table were found at an antiques fair.

stove, give an element of traditional country style to this otherwise modern setting. Behind the Aga is a scullery with a wall of cupboards, the refrigerator and a deep sink.

On the far side of the kitchen is the Garden Room, the office where Graham and Richard administer National Trust business. The back stairs, floors and steps at this side of the house have been painted in a mix of red and black paint that has been blended to a shade of deep brown. This not only gives a grounding to the otherwise white-painted areas but also echoes the deep colour of the old timbers found throughout the house.

At the top of the back stairs are two guest bedrooms, simply decorated with white walls and crisp white bedlinen. Between the second guest bedroom and the bathroom, a door opens to a dressing room with one wall of fitted wardrobes, and beyond this is the main bedroom.

Although this room has a low central beam and is not tall, it feels spacious because it is wide. Once again insulating duvet curtains have been employed to keep winter gales at bay. A round table and two bedside tables, recently found at an antiques market at a racecourse, have been added.

On the far side of the small front landing by the main bedroom is another bathroom, with a roll top bath fitted in neatly between beams and rafters. Stairs lead down from this landing to the main entrance and the Great Hall.

Beyond the Great Hall there is a private library where Graham has a wall of shelves filled with gardening books and a drawing board where he designs the garden layouts, and Richard has an easel where he paints portraits.

Although there is a distinct division between the public and private spaces in this house, there is one room where the two meet. After hours, when the doors and gates are closed and the National Trust visitors have gone home, there are occasions when the long wooden table in the Great Hall is dressed with white linen and sparkling glass, and dinner is served in stately style.

local inspiration

Bradley Gardner and his wife Debbie came to Bali and bought a plot of land on a promontory by the 'mother of Balinese rivers', the Ayung. Here they built a holiday home in traditional style with open sides and a thatched roof, where the elements not only play an important part in the daily running of the house but have also inspired its decoration.

LEFT: The Gardners' house, Windsong is entered by stepping onto a stone set in a lake of waterlilies and goldfish. Beyond the sitting area on this upper level is an open dining room and the master suite.

The Gardners' home, Bayugita or Windsong, was designed, with the help of Malaysian architect Cheong Yew Kuan, to be a house without boundaries, where home is in the garden and the garden is part of the home. The site, on the edge of a hill, is fanned by gentle breezes, which pass through the open sides and verandas of the main living area and are scented by the flowers of the frangipani and jasmine trees that have been planted around it.

The timber-framed house with a thatched alang-alang roof is reached by a bridge-like stepping stone set into the lily pond that surrounds the house and makes it appear like an island. Visitors take off their shoes, as if going into a temple, and walk barefoot on the smooth warm wood of the floor or wear the banana-leaf slippers provided.

Where possible, recycled and ecologically sound materials were used in the construction of the house and regional customs were observed. Much of the excavation and building was done by hand, and local products such as coconut shells, cut and polished and made into decorative ceiling tiles, were incorporated into the scheme. Finely woven palm matting has been applied to many surfaces, for example as backing for the roof timbers and as panel facing. Much of the wood has been reclaimed from old buildings, and if new wood has been used it has come from managed forests.

To furnish the spacious living area of Windsong with its richly coloured, polished wood floors and breathtaking jungle aspect, Debbie found local craftsmen, of whom there are many on the island as carving is a local craft, to create specific pieces. A long lounging sofa which takes up much of the width of the seating area, a low, generous-size oblong coffee table and Bergere-style chairs, which mix local carving in solid wood with woven wicker backs, were among the required commissions.

Hand-dyed batik from Java, printed in muted shades of natural indigo and soft pink on a white cotton background, has been used for cushion covers. Other decorative objects and carpets, many antique, were collected by Debbie on her frequent travels around Southeast Asia from their main home in Hong Kong .

Also in the spacious living room is a dining area, with a long teak table and chairs. A sideboard rests in front of the balustrades of the staircase that leads down to the lower level. On this floor is the study, kitchen and further bedrooms and bathrooms, and also access to the swimming pool.

Double doors at the far end of the sitting and dining room open to the master bedroom, panelled in recycled wood. A copy of a Venetian bed is swathed in tented furls of fine cotton muslin and covered with a lightly quilted Javanese batik throw and crisp white bedlinen.

From the bedroom a set of double doors, to the right of the bedhead, leads to a dressing room which is dominated by a locally constructed wardrobe. In a separate room to the side of the wardrobe an original English Victorian lavatory and handbasin have been plumbed.

Beside the dressing room is the main bathroom, which opens to the garden on two sides but can be made more private by dropping down two huge bamboo blinds. The handbasin, shower and large oval bath are formed from a composite material flecked with slivers of shimmering mother-of-pearl shell that reflect the island nature of the location. Outside, a Jacuzzi bath is positioned in the walled garden under the boughs of a frangipani tree whose scented blooms drop into the bubbling water.

Once Windsong was complete, the Gardners decided to build four more houses on the twenty-acre (eight-hectare) plot, which they landscaped with water gardens and plantations of coconuts and flamboyant plants. Following on

with their theme of the elements, the next house to be constructed was Tirta Ening or Clear Water, built from *ening batu* or golden stone and some 150-year-old wood that was discovered buried on a neighbouring island.

Tejasuara, or House of the Sound of Fire, has a primitive, earthy feel and is constructed from stone imported from the eastern island of Sumba, recycled ironwood telegraph poles and a native hardwood, merbau. Wanakasa, the Forest in the Mist house, is at the point of the promontory among the jungle of trees. The fifth building, Umabona or House of the Earth Son, has a scheme of wood, stone and bamboo.

By respecting the environment and working with local craftsmen and materials, the Gardners have constructed houses, and especially their own home, that have a truly harmonious and ethnic feel, reflecting the local culture and a style of living that is best suited to the climate. They have also managed to incorporate many of the modern facilities that make living on a tropical island such as Bali an even more enjoyable experience.

ABOVE: Outdoor bathing is a part of daily life in Bali, and the Gardners' Jacuzzi, in a shell-composite sculpted bath, is in their walled garden under the branches of a frangipani tree.

RIGHT: In the main suite the bed is draped with fine muslin so that doors and windows can be left open at night and soft breezes can cool the room. The bed is dressed with batik prints.

FAR LEFT: The imposing staircase leads from the foyer of the main hall up to the first floor. Although of modern construction, its shape, grandeur and elegance echo that of a time gone by.

LEFT: Looking from the top of the staircase, the view is of both the lower level and upper levels. Below, the long passageway leads to the kitchen and informal sitting room. Upstairs on the right is the spacious master suite.

hollywood glamour

Jules Haimovitz, a native New Yorker, started his career at Radio City Music Hall. Having worked on TV shows such as *The Cosby Show* and *Roseanne*, he went on to become President of Metro-Goldwyn-Mayer Networks. He lives off Mulholland Drive in Beverly Hills, in a modern house that has been built to convey classic Hollywood style.

Jules Haimovitz bought a two-acre (one-hectare) plot of land in a hillside development because of the privacy it would provide. On one side is a game reserve and on the other are banks of trees. The rear of the house has uninterrupted views of the San Fernando Valley and beyond.

Jules worked with Los Angeles architect Larry Scheiderer and New York designer Richard Mervis to create a home that, although new, has a feeling of vintage glamour. Jules has an empathy with Art Deco style and the straight lines and distinct shapes that can be seen in great New York buildings such as the Empire State and Radio City.

Although the land was purchased in 1989, the project suffered a series of delays, the most major being the earthquake of 1994. Jules was in New York on business but on his return saw the after-effects and got his architect to

RIGHT: The formal sitting room mixes classic pieces of 1930s furniture with modern pieces by the Parisian designer Christian Liaigre, which have the same angular lines. The strong California sunlight is diffused by light hand-stitched silk chiffon curtains on the long windows which, to the left, look out on the San Fernando Valley.

RIGHT: Along one wall of the wood-panelled study is a custom-made desk and behind it a banquette seat. The Amboynas wood chairs made in the 1930s originally sat in the Press Club in Paris.

redesign the house with a 'quake-resistant' basement. Within this subterranean space is a private screening room, a kitchen, a bar and, at the far end, a games room with snooker table. Steps lead up the outside of this area past the guest cottage to the tennis court, swimming pool and Jacuzzi.

Inside, an elevator with trompe l'oeil panelling silently glides up to the ground floor and a long limestone corridor. To the left are the staff quarters. To the right are the steel-and-blond-wood kitchen with a wall of glass-fronted refrigerators, and the breakfast room with huge windows overlooking the terrace. A graceful archway, boarded with a stepped architrave, leads through to the family room and bar. The side wall has folding glass panels that open onto the terrace, enabling the bar to be accessed from both indoors and out. The remaining

walls are covered with pale brown raw linen, and much of the furniture is by French designer Christian Liaigre. In the dramatic main hallway a life-size Burmese Buddha sits close to an eggshell-and-gold-leaf four-screen panel made in 1925. Beyond the gold Deco screen is Jules's mahogany-panelled study. Here the furnishings are simple but magnificent and include a pair of Amboynas wood chairs, circa 1930, from the Paris Press Club. A custom-made desk runs along the side of the room in front of an ecru suede upholstered banquette, where Jules likes to recline when he works.

Back in the hallway an oval lantern window illuminates the grand staircase, which finishes between two imposing angular pillars. On the far side of the hall is the octagonal dining room. To the side of the dining room is the living room.

Pieces of Deco furniture, such as the 1930s French armchairs by Michel Dufet, ebony coffee table with eggshell details and cabinet by Primavera, sit on a silk-and-linen rug. To the left of the marble fire surround hangs a lithograph by Jean Cocteau. On the built-in shelving on either side of the steps that lead down to the living room are two 1930s Ato clocks. At the windows, curtains in bechamel wool and blond silk chiffon diffuse the California sunlight. Amid the vintage furniture are more contemporary pieces by Christian Liaigre.

In the front hall Jules had a number of tall walk-in cupboards built. One contains all the workings of the house's complex sound system. Another, inspired by a visit to the Playboy Mansion, is a soundproof phone booth.

The first floor has two guest suites to the front and Jules's suite runs across the full width of the rear of the house. This contains a separate 'partner's' bathroom and dressing room with vast walk-in wardrobe. Next is a small sitting room with banquettes and, beyond, a palatial bedroom dominated by a custom-built bed by Dakota Jackson. Along part of one wall is a buttermilk suede-covered sofa by Carolyn Lawrence and a pair of armchairs from a Paris flea market. On either side of the bed are custom-made nightstands, and two large glass-and-wood screens are placed beside the bedhead. Beyond the bedroom on the far side is Jules's dressing room and bathroom which lead through to a fully equipped gym.

Jules's Hollywood home reflects the past with its classic style, and the decor owes much to a bygone era of glamour.

ABOVE: The formal angular dining room, off the main entrance hall, has seating arranged around an octagonal wood table. This table is constructed in sections so that it can be enlarged or reduced by adding or subtracting segment-type panels.

grand style

Internationally renowned cello soloist Mischa Maisky, a pupil of both Mstislav Rostropovich at the Moscow Conservatoire and the Russian emigré cellist Gregor Piatigotsk, lives in a house designed by Art Nouveau architect Victor Horta outside Brussels, with his wife Kay and their two children. The house combines the flowing lines of Horta's original design with more ornate additions introduced by a subsequent owner of the house in the 1940s.

LEFT: The terrace that was an external feature of the house in Horta's time was subsequently enclosed and is now the temperature-controlled music room where Maisky and his family practise. The view from this elevated site is of the countryside near La Hulpe.

The Maiskys' home is in a forested domain on the invisible line between the French- and Flemish-speaking parts of Belgium. The family moved to the area thirteen years ago from Paris, and lived nearby until they came across their current home.

Surrounded by woodland, the imposing three-storey house is almost invisible, except in winter when the leaves fall, but once seen it is never forgotten. It was built in 1908 by the Belgian architect Victor Horta, who founded the Art Nouveau movement; its style is a simplified version of haute Art Nouveau, which is known for its curling organic shapes and decorative carved stonework. Here Horta opted for cleaner lines and shapes but still employed much of the wrought ironwork that is so much a part of that period's style.

The house was sold in the 1940s, and the subsequent owner enclosed many of the outside terraces and added elaborate decoration and murals on the inside. This decoration includes Lalique-style glass panels in the doors, inset details in the marble floors, and applied copper and gilded embellishments to the staircase. Much of this decor depicts mermaids and seahorses, alluding to the fact that the

ABOVE: The dining room is on a level raised slightly above the hallway and is reached by a short flight of steps. The imposing fireplace and seahorse chandelier date from the 1940s when additional decoration was added to the original Horta house.

house is built on the point where six springs meet. Other decorations, such as the murals on the staircase, appropriately show themes that depict, for example, musicians and musical instruments.

Kay, with the help of local architect Ferdinand Joachim, spent three years reviving the beautiful old house. The Maiskys did not interfere with the existing features, but used colour to soften some of the more dominant elements of the decor and to unify the diverse aspects and numerous rooms.

From the circular ground-floor vestibule, with its dark-blue domed ceiling, you walk into the black marble hallway and past the mural-painted walls of the staircase which sweeps grandly up to the first floor. At the end of the hallway on the left, a brief set of steps rises to the dining area with its deep, ornately carved stone fireplace.

Beside a long baronial-style dining table is a bay with window seats and a breakfast table used by the family for less

formal meals. The view from the tall windows to the back of the room is over the forest to the valley and lake below.

Opposite the dining room, to the right of the hallway, is the salon, a small reception area with an unusual fireplace beneath a window. The fireplace is unusual because it has no central chimney or breast, the flue from the fire being ducted around the side of the window frame. Through an arch from the salon is the library, once an outside terrace, and one of the rooms created when the house was bought from Horta.

The other room that was enclosed at that time is the semi-circular piano room which lies immediately in front of the hallway. This room, with a marble floor and decoratively panelled ceiling, is fitted with electronic blinds to protect the grand piano from direct sunlight and four humidifiers to keep moisture at the correct level.

On the first floor is another small library, and beyond is Mischa's study. In the study, opaque glass-fronted cabinets

filled with musical scores line one wall, and in the centre there is a small podium and a chair where the maestro practises his cello. In the bay window to the front of the house is an office with computers and faxes spilling out requests and arrangements for yet another international round of musical performances.

Next door to the study is the family room with French doors opening onto a deck on the roof of the piano room below. The walls of this room are panelled, but most conceal cupboards filled with CDs, tapes and videos.

The spacious master bedroom is to the side of the house over the dining room, and is decorated with wooden panelling and soft coloured contemporary upholstery and bed throws. The bathroom is decorated in period-style mint-green tiles with a border of zigzag-patterned navy blue and gold tiles. A staircase beside the room leads to the childrens' and guest rooms above.

The roof of the top floor was raised during Kay's readjustments to the house, to give more light and space to what were previously servants' quarters. A new staircase, with a contemporary but curling Art Nouveau-style wrought-iron balustrade, winds up past sky-blue walls painted with trompe l'oeil clouds.

Maisky's musical travels have also helped in the decorative restoration of the house. Mischa was playing a concert at the Smetner Hall in Prague when he looked up and saw the light fittings. He realized that they were ideal for the salon and hallway of his home so tracked down a local company and had them copied.

The Maisky family have created a unique home in a house that is rich in history. In doing this they have managed to maintain and consolidate the work and influence of two previous owners yet incorporate the needs and requirements of a modern and musically talented family, all under one roof.

CENTRE: Another of the enclosed terraces is now a library with an ornate mother-of-pearl inlaid cabinet. This room has an intimate and cosy feel. Being to the side of the house, it is less bright, but it still has views over the forest below.

ABOVE: This section of the main staircase shows a small part of the mural that covers the walls up to the first floor landing. The stairs are also bordered by highly decorative gilded balustrades.

contemporary

PREVIOUS PAGES: Maria's minimalist bedroom has a sumptuously covered bed and a bedside stool-cum-table.

LEFT: In the spacious open-plan living room the grand piano is easily accommodated. A specially made, curving red sofa sits in front of the windows.

the party place

Self-taught fashion designer Maria Grachvogel worked for some time in banking to finance the establishment of her own couture label, which she founded in 1991. Fans of her glamorous and flattering clothes include singer Victoria Beckham and actress Emma Thompson. Her central London apartment is a strictly modern venue, minimally but dramatically furnished with colourful and curvaceous contemporary designs.

Maria Grachvogel and her fiancé Mike Simcock are not averse to a little glamour in their lives, and the apartment they share on the second and third floor of a block near Marylebone Road in central London has been designed with parties and entertaining in mind.

The apartment is part of a comparatively recent construction built in the 1950s on a World War II bomb site. It was constructed so that the facade matched the rest of the period terrace, but inside it was designed to be used specifically as offices.

As the rooms had been only recently and rudimentarily converted from offices to a residential space, the finish and detailing was basic, but this appealed to Maria and Mike so they bought the apartment. They removed the few renovations and additions that had been added, including skirting boards, flooring and door handles. Once they had created a clean shell, they set about dividing up the space.

With entertaining in mind, they kept the main living area open-plan, so that they can accommodate up to 120 people as well as Mike's grand piano. A curving glass cocktail bar, which is lit from beneath so that it appears to glow, adds to the glamour.

The steel-clad kitchen is equipped with concealed spice drawers, a barbecue grill and a large refrigerator with integral ice-maker, which is essential for the cocktail hour. Small glass shelves up the wall above the bar area contain an array of Martini and shot glasses, as well as colourful bottles of liqueurs and spirits, all of which add to the colour and sparkle of the decor.

The attractive cocktail bar doubles as a more informal breakfast bar in the morning. Its ritzy appearance hides its very practical role in dividing the large room into a more regular, oblong and manageable size without detaching or cutting off the kitchen. Daylight from the window at the back of the kitchen also helps to illuminate the bar area during the day.

On the other side of the bar is a dining table and chairs made from metal twig-and-branch-like supports from Bali. The couple also commissioned a matching table base. Once the base was safely installed in the flat, they ordered a glass panel for the table top, and when it was delivered it was so heavy that it took four men to carry the plate-glass section up the stairs.

The rest of the room is furnished with a well-polished black grand piano on which Mike plays jazz and classical music, a red, curving two-piece sofa and a long lilac daybed. The latter pieces of furniture were specially made to order so that they would be of the right generous proportions to suit the space, and their curves counteract the angles and openness of the room.

The colourful paintings, including works by Charlotte Valeur, hang on the wall by the piano. The long, wall-mounted column radiators were chosen specially to be a decorative feature in their own right and, together with the paintings, against the plain white walls create an almost gallery-like feel in the spacious, uncluttered room.

On the way to the staircase, which goes up to the second floor, there is a small cloakroom with an opaque glass door and a basin supported on a chrome coil. Here again glass has been used to provide practical surfaces which look graphic and stylish even in this utilitarian space. Carrying on up the stairs, passing a huge, framed Prêt-à-Porter fashion poster and beneath an overhead lightwell, you arrive in a small

LEFT: This view from the bedroom through to the corridor and guest bathroom beyond gives an indication of the depth and size of the apartment. In the bedroom a Verner Panton chair sits to the right of the sliding, opaque glass doors that enclose the slate-clad bathroom.

RIGHT: Behind the opaque glass door at the bottom of the staircase is the lower-level cloakroom. It has an eye-catching spring-base support and glass handbasin set in front of a raised glass shelf.

FAR RIGHT: Dividing the kitchen from the dining and main living space is the up-lit cocktail bar. This is both a practical as well as a decorative feature and helps to contain and define the two spaces.

corridor with polished wood floors. To the left is the door to the extensive main bedroom. An L-shape of fitted wardrobes with opaque glass doors takes up one and a half walls of the bedroom. Another pair of opaque glass doors slides back to reveal a modern but earthy slate-clad bathroom with a luxurious Jacuzzi bath, spacious walk-in shower enclosure and a matching pair of his-and-hers handbasins.

The minimally furnished bedroom features a large bed, draped with sumptuous, rich purple and intense burgundy velvet throws. The remaining pieces of furniture include a bright pink Verner Panton multi-functional recliner seat and a stool with spidery steel legs that doubles as a bedside table.

At the other end of the corridor is a small study, a spare bedroom and another bathroom. The fittings in this bathroom are all white with a long-necked, floor-standing spout to convey water into the tub. Iridescent halogen lightbulbs give the white fittings a pearlized pink effect, which makes them more interesting and less clinical than would the use of standard lighting.

This clean-cut contemporary home creates a perfect setting for dramatically shaped modern furniture and vivid pieces of artwork. The interesting use of glass and the clever use of space make even service areas such as the kitchen and cloakroom places of style and interest.

LEFT: This section of the main open-plan living area shows the dining space with kitchen beyond and the staircase to the mezzanine. The windows overlook the Tate Modern, the Millennium Bridge and the River Thames.

RIGHT: On the curving mezzanine there is a private sitting area with two chaises longues on a wide balcony section outside the main bedroom. At this level there are magnificent views through the windows set into the adjacent walls.

skyline views

When they arrived in London from Sweden, Kristina Borjesson and her husband chose to live in the South Bank area by the River Thames, where they were able to watch the development of two of the city's new landmarks, the Tate Modern art gallery and the Millennium Bridge. Here they have transformed a basic shell apartment into a light and modern functional home that combines open areas with more intimate spaces.

living room by a curved glass-brick wall, which allows light from the main room to illuminate the windowless hallway but obscures the view on either side. It also contains the coat-and-boot cupboard and provides a physical break between the outside world and the inner sanctum. On the other side of the glass wall the spacious living area is arranged in the shape of a back-to-front L-shape. The kitchen is at the top end of the letter, a dining area along the long back, and in the foot is the small, more formal sitting area.

The fresh, blue-green painted kitchen runs across the width of the end wall and has splashbacks of opaque reinforced glass. The glass is visually sympathetic to the watery location, and also reflects and amplifies the daylight that pours in through the long wall of windows that runs along the whole side wall of the building. Skylights, like those above a ship's hold, are set into an upwardly curved, pale yellow ceiling and ensure that there is plenty of light in the preparation and cooking areas. Although comparatively small, the kitchen is well planned and is often used to produce meals for up to twenty-five people.

Kristina worked for the Swedish Design and Craft Association and has used many pieces of Swedish and Danish design to decorate the apartment. Some are student designs, others from well-known companies. For example, in the dining area a custom-made glass-topped table is surrounded by wooden bucket chairs with vivid terra-cotta upholstery that matches the colour of the seats on the chrome-legged Arne Jacobsen chairs. A cherrywood sideboard rests along the wall by the hall door supporting a collection of glass bowls and glasses, some by Kosta Boda. When it came to choosing colours for the walls, Kristina worked with a painter who trained at the German Steiner School. He mixed and applied them in a special way so that in areas where there is plenty of light the colours are lighter, while in the corners they become darker and more intense. Each wall has subtle variations in tone which emphasize the shapes through the different areas.

From the dining area a curving metal-and-wood staircase, with a noticeable ship-like quality, leads up to the mezzanine and around the outer walls of a tapered funnel-like column, which houses the kitchen pantry at the lower level and a walk-in wardrobe above.

On the upper level, overlooking the kitchen, is a compact study. As you follow the mezzanine round, it widens and opens out into a small, more intimate sitting room and library with ample chaises longues of contemporary design. This section overlooks part of the formal sitting area below, where antique chairs are mixed with small modern sofas, low

The Borjessons bought their fifth floor apartment as a shell, with just the outer walls, a concrete floor and the roof, and set about dividing it up into a living space. At first they didn't want to have any internal walls, but finally decided that some were needed to create privacy for visitors. So a self-contained guest area with two bedrooms and a bathroom was located on the far side of the entrance hall.

The hall and guest spaces are separated from the main

FAR LEFT: The small but well-designed kitchen and breakfast bar is set against a pale watery-blue-painted wall with a reinforced opaque glass splashback protecting the wall at the lower level. Above on the mezzanine is a compact study.

LEFT: The curvaceous metal staircase has a nautical appearance as though rising to the upper deck of a ship. It passes in front of the glass brick wall which separates the hall, two guest bedrooms and large shower room from the main living area.

coffee tables and display cases of glass and ceramics. Double-height arched windows provide those sitting at either level with ample daylight and views of life on the River Thames.

Behind the cosy upper-level sitting room is the master bedroom, simply furnished with concealed cupboards. There are two bathrooms. The one en suite is streamlined and business-like, a place to wash first thing in the morning. The other bathroom, downstairs, has a large walk-in shower with a built-in tiled seat so that you can sit or lie down and relax in the water and the steam.

The Borjessons' home has a subtle but not overpowering reference to its warehouse location and nautical outlook. The exposed metal beams and tall ceiling, and the curved metal and wood staircase all allude to more utilitarian roots, but the fine detailing, subtle colouring and elegant furniture make it a pleasurable and sophisticated contemporary urban dwelling.

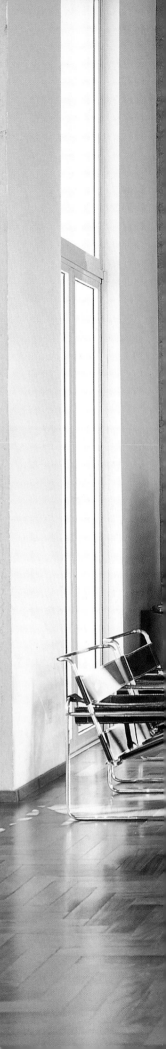

RIGHT: Carlos Miele on his Le Corbusier recliner in the seating area, which is furnished with other classic designer chairs. This area is focused around the wall of recycled brick and a simple contemporary hearth with an organ-pipe-like chimney. The warm colouring of the brick and wooden floor help to soften the angular lines.

latin living

Carlos Miele is one of South America's hottest and sexiest fashion designers. The clothes he creates are sensuous, made in molten-metal mail, lacy laser-cut leather, stretch chamois and exotic feathers that undulate and slide over each dip of the body. Yet his home is minimal, angular, almost hard, with bare brickwork and a tall, cathedral-like living space.

In the heart of São Paulo's Itaim Bibi district, Carlos Miele has an eyrie-like loft apartment on the fifteenth and sixteenth floors of a building constructed by his brothers' company. Having fired four different architects for his home, he finally supervised the design himself, and the result is a cool, calculated, pared-down penthouse.

Internally, the construction of the cathedral-high living space is in 'raw' materials such as bare concrete and giant panes of glass and brick, while the use of warm red brick and wooden floors give some relief to the strict monotone scheme. On this upper level there are no curtains or blinds and the space is open-plan. This accentuates its vastness and also allows daylight from the glass windows and walls to filter through to the centre. Balconies, reached by pairs of glass-panelled doors, run around most of this level. Doors also open from a small rear gym space to a pebble mosaic deck and hot tub, and at the far end of the deck more doors lead back to the far corner of the living space and a simple bed dressed with crisp white sheets. The only colourful decoration here is provided by a select choice of objects: poles of carved wooden birds, baskets of brightly coloured beads and carved gourds, and a magnificent red-and-blue feathered headdress.

RIGHT: The skyline of São Paulo is a dramatic setting for the pebble mosaic and the hot tub on the deck of Carlos Miele's sixteenth-floor home.

FAR RIGHT: The internal curving concrete wall, which contains a bathroom, in the otherwise open-plan upper living level.

All these unusual decorative objects are the work of native rainforest Indians.

At the far side of the room is the main seating area, grouped around the hearth and wall made from salvaged bricks. The furniture is made up of classic pieces, selected because Miele admires the designers' work. There is a Le Corbusier sofa, chair and recliner, and a couple of Marcel Breuer chairs with their original leather seats. Halfway along the outer wall, between the seating area and the bed, is another recliner, this one a Mies van der Rohe design. Opposite, on the back of the curving internal wall which contains a small bathroom, is a music centre and stacks of CDs.

To the side of the seating area, on the other side of the staircase, is the dining room and adjacent small kitchen and bar. None of these spaces show signs of wear because Miele, living in the heart of the city near its best restaurants and clubs, often goes out to dine, and when he does stay in he orders take-out sushi. The antique Portuguese shell-carved dining chairs and glass table resting on two old carved-wood pillars prove to be decorative rather than essential.

The wood-tread stairs lead to the lower floor and a collection of smaller, more intimate rooms. On either side of the master bedroom are en suite bathrooms and individual dressing areas. Miele's side of the room is filled with a rail of clothes and shoes, and two modern chests of drawers on top of which are stacks of folded jeans.

The pristine white bathrooms are sparse and hotel-like, with oval, white Jacuzzi baths placed in front of the windows and counter-sunk handbasins. Bars of soap, still in their packaging, are stacked up beside bottles of mineral water and piles of freshly laundered white towels. At the end of the corridor outside the bedroom is another small sitting room, with two large velvet-covered armchairs with ribbed conical legs, and a daybed.

Miele regards his home as a very private space. It is also the antithesis of his colourful and flamboyant fashion designs. It is where he comes home after an evening out to read and to work. He says that his best, most creative hours are from 1 to 4 A.M., then he goes to bed and sleeps until late in the morning.

LEFT: A classic sofa upholstered with calico and draped with a sequined ethnic throw sits on the painted floor of the first floor sitting room, beside a contemporary plastic-covered chair.

RIGHT: Part of Joseph's collection of antlers and horns is arranged on the sitting room wall above a picture by Sam Taylor Wood, a gift from the artist to her friend Serena.

above the shop

Business and domestic partners Joseph Corre and Serena Rees are the heads of the international decadent lingerie company Agent Provocateur. They work and live with their young daughter Cora in a listed building dating from 1750, near the City of London's Smithfield meat market. Their home mirrors their colourful and exotic taste and their interest in contemporary furniture design.

RIGHT: An old, mottled mirror reflects the kitchen table and chairs and the exotic 1940s print on the end wall. Beyond the kitchen is the fireplace and one of the large front windows of the sitting room.

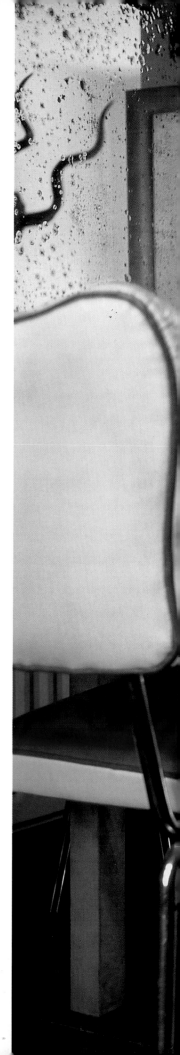

The home that the Corre family has created is on three floors above the original Agent Provocateur showroom on the ground floor and their basement offices and design studio. Because of the building's age and listed status, any alterations or improvements had to be approved by the appropriate authorities who insisted, among other things, that the distinctive double carriage doors at ground level be retained.

When Joseph and Serena bought the building it was in a dilapidated state and took time to repair. In the past the building had been used as a meat store, and on two levels the floors sloped so that blood and water could drain away.

Unlike others in the traditional City area who have opted for single-room, loft-style homes, Joseph and Serena decided to keep the smaller individual rooms on each floor, and thus retained the character and period feel of this unique building.

From the narrow, private front door to their home, which is beside the main double doors of the office, a coat-lined corridor takes you to a steep flight of stairs leading to a small half-landing. Here there is a cloakroom and lavatory with silver-and-red Chinese-style wallpaper that the couple designed themselves and had specially printed.

Previously the first floor had been a store and office space, but Joseph and Serena made it into a living room and kitchen, with a dining area which opens out onto the roof terrace at the back.

In the living room there is a long sofa unit made by the contemporary Italian design company Edra, which Joseph and Serena represent in the UK. This leather-covered seat is placed across the width of the room under the deep, prune-brown painted window frames and sills. The back sections of the sofa are multi-adjustable and can be turned round and bent to create smaller armchair-like arrangements on the base.

The prune-brown paint colour used on the window frames and external doors was carefully researched by the couple and is an authentic Georgian colour which is appropriate to the age of the building. But elsewhere in the living room the decoration is more contemporary.

Posters of the punk band The Sex Pistols hanging over the fireplace, and also in the hallways, are a reminder of Joseph's childhood. His parents are the fashion designer Vivienne Westwood and record producer Malcolm McClaren, one-time manager of the band. Along the wall opposite the fireplace and poster is Joseph's steadily growing collection of mounted antlers and horns, which has expanded to include a pair of matching horn chairs. Echoing the horn theme is the cowhide rug stretched out over the black-painted wooden floor. Underneath the display of horns is a framed picture specially done for Serena by her friend the acclaimed artist Sam Taylor Wood. A calico-covered, classic-style two-seater sofa draped with an ethnic sequined throw sits by the opening to the kitchen and beside it is a contemporary white plastic-covered box chair. A long low coffee table in front of the multi-adjustable lounging sofa completes the furnishings in this room.

The kitchen is a small and busy room. Glass-fronted cupboards are filled with stacks of unmatched plates and glasses. Examples of Cora's artwork are pinned on the wall by the bright red refrigerator, and saucepans and cooking pots hang from butcher's hooks suspended from the ceiling. Padded and piped 1950s-style American diner chairs with shining chrome legs are arranged around a plain wood kitchen table. An old speckled-silver mirror reflects light back over diners from the main windows in the living room and the French doors that lead to the roof terrace on the other side. A 1940s framed picture of a painted pin-up holding exotic fruits adds an unexpected flash of colour and a reminder of the titillating business that this couple run from the floors beneath their home.

On the landing outside the sitting-room door a vivid red chair appears to have been covered by the contents of a giant dish of spaghetti pomodoro as thick coils of bright red rope curl around the chair to create comfortable padding over the metal frame. Stairs from here lead up to the top two floors where there are three bedrooms, two bathrooms and a dressing room.

Joseph and Serena have successfully contained their quirky and contemporary sense of style within the narrow confines of a Georgian building on the edges of London's main meat market. Although both are noted for their modern attitude to style, they nevertheless enjoy the sense of community and a history dating back through centuries.

calm simplicity

Fashion designer Anna Valentine of Robinson Valentine creates classic clothes with a contemporary edge for customers including Serena Linley, opera singer Dame Kiri Te Kawana and actress Emily Watson. Her home is similar: colour and design are simple, with accessories used to enhance the appearance. The result is a calm, clear home with restful Zen-like qualities.

LEFT: The plain white walls, undecorated fireplace and simple painted floor of the main bedroom provide a blank canvas against which the furnishings and accessories set a style and create a mood.

BELOW: Raw plaster walls in a warm terra-cotta shade give a Mediterranean feel to the kitchen. This feeling is enhanced by the unfussy wooden units and open shelves bearing basketware and pots of fresh herbs.

There is a peaceful order in the west London home of Anna Valentine and her husband Jonathan Berger. The three-storey, end-of-terrace house is simply furnished in an understated, timeless way but with touches of Oriental and Mediterranean influences.

The house is not decorated to comply with any specific category of style. It is more a mix of things that Anna and Jonathan feel comfortable with. With their busy lifestyles, Anna believes that 'simplicity creates calm'.

After the couple bought their home they spent eight months working with builders to create the perfect shell before adding the decoration. They opted for the simplest basis for the decoration, choosing white paint for most of the rooms.

The ground floor has a long living/dining area with French doors opening out onto the garden. This open-plan room contains two period fireplaces, one at each end, and a plain, polished wooden floor runs throughout. Over the mantel in the dining area a large mirror reflects light from the windows directly opposite. The simple furnishings include a wooden table surrounded by traditional chairs and a tall unit stacked with CDs.

The windows of the living area are covered with adjustable calico blinds that Anna designed so that they can be used to screen the lower half of the window, leaving the upper half open. A small two-seater sofa sits in the recess of the bow window and adjacent to it is another sofa. On the wall above the second sofa there is a tranquil blue painting contrasting with a fiery red one in the hall, both by Tom Hammick. There is also a painting by Alistair Robinson, another of whose works is in the kitchen. The rest of the furnishings and accessories in the living room have Oriental origins. A low futon mat is stretched out like a rug in front of

FAR LEFT: For the windows at the sitting-room end of the main room, the calico blinds close down to the sill in the evening, giving privacy, but the upper sections, which are above eye-level, can be left open.

LEFT: This view from the sitting section of the room looks through to the classic fireplace and furnishings of the dining area. The large mirror over the mantel reflects the light and view from the windows opposite.

the fire, a carved Indonesian daybed topped with a sheet of glass has been converted into a coffee table, while an eastern carved wood cabinet stores clutter.

Outside, beyond the French doors in the dining room, lies the garden. In the part nearest these rooms there is a small, contemplative angular pond and a headless statue of Buddha bordered by exotic shrubs and more Oriental artefacts. But further on the mood changes, and lavender and other herbs create a feel of Provence. In the kitchen, which lies beyond the dining room, the decoration continues this Mediterranean feel with walls of terracotta plaster, simple fitted wood units and accessories such as baskets and pots of fresh herbs.

From the hallway that runs alongside the sitting and dining area, stairs lead up to the first floor. At the top of the stairs is the bathroom where the theme reverts to the Oriental. The walls are painted a rich saffron yellow and along the side of the bath is a carved wood panel from Indonesia; in the corner by the windowsill sits a carved stone Buddha's head.

From the bathroom a further, short flight of stairs leads up to a small landing. To the left is the spare bedroom which is predominantly white. Behind the door a light wood chest has been made by stacking three separate units on top of each other. Against the minimalist background, decoration is provided by antique beaded bags, a rich red silk shawl and a tall freestanding mirror that reflects tea-light candles in glass holders resting on the floor at its base.

Further along the upper hallway to the front of the house is the main bedroom, again with white walls and white-painted floorboards. For the three long windows which overlook the street below, Anna has used another clever blind design. This device is a simple calico tabard attached to the lower rail of a coathanger which hangs from the upper surround of the window frames. Just off the bedroom is the en suite bathroom, again white and simply decorated.

This simply decorated house allows the accessories and furnishings to create the mood in each room.

Scandinavian style

Karl Edholm supports design by collecting classic pieces in his capacious lakeside home on the outskirts of Stockholm, and also by developing new classics for the future. He and his wife Marie left their advertising company to set up Mect, a business that promotes Nordic design. Their modern three-level house is the perfect setting for an enviable collection of original twentieth-century designs.

RIGHT: The view from the upper living area, through the lower section towards the hall and front door, shows the two levels and, to the left, the stairs that go down to the main bedroom.

FOLLOWING PAGES: The upper level of the main living room has an unhindered view of the lake. This part of the house is furnished with many pieces of modern classic design by Alvar Aalto, Achille Castiglioni and Charles Eames.

Karl and Marie Edholm's house, built in 1971 and designed by a Danish architect, is ideal in size and style for the modern furniture that graphic designer Karl first started to collect thirty years ago.

At that time he bought pieces as he came across them rather than through dealers or specialists. Among his early purchases was an Alvar Aalto chair; then he added a Castiglioni Arco light. The Eames chair he bought eight years later in New York, where he was working in an advertising agency. When Karl started to collect this furniture it was not very popular; it had been new and innovative but, as with many fashions, its time had passed and most people were putting it out of their homes rather than bringing it in.

When Karl and his family moved to this house, his collection of now highly desirable furniture found a perfect setting. The open rooms, the end wall of glass in the sitting room and the simple panelled ceilings do not detract from or compete with the graphic shapes and designer lines of the furniture. If anything, they enhance it and show it off to its best advantage.

It was the setting of the house itself, rather than the setting it would provide for the furniture collection, that first attracted the Edholms. On the outskirts of Stockholm, the

house sits on the edge of a lake where the family swim, boat and fish in the summer and ice-skate in the winter.

When they bought the house they had to extend the original building to provide more space for their family. This included wing sections on either side of the house, and a deck and outdoor living area to the back. Now tailored to suit both their needs and those of the furniture collection, it is something of a twentieth-century showcase.

From the front door you walk into a wide hallway with a cloak and shower room to one side. Beyond the hall is a large split-level living area reached by a small flight of polished wooden steps. On the lower level in this room are the kitchen and breakfast space, the main wall of which is dominated by a Miro-like painting done by an artist for one of their previous company's advertising campaigns. Under the spacecraft-style Poul Henningsen light, an angular bench table is surrounded by black Arne Jacobsen chairs.

The white kitchen is well equipped with the latest in Scandinavian design and gadgets. A waist-height breakfast bar divides the cooking and casual eating spaces but allows the natural light from windows on both sides of the house to reach the centre of the building.

On the upper level, the sitting room is furnished with more classic pieces, a list of which reads like a guide to a contemporary furniture museum. There are Verner Panton chairs at the formal round dining table, and these chairs are even more exceptional because they are still in their original orange covers.

A timeless Eames chair and ottoman in rosewood-faced moulded plywood sit next to two Alvar Aalto birch-frame and bent-plywood chairs with webbing backs and seats, and a trolley by the same designer. Two Castiglioni Arco lamps curve gracefully to the ceiling and back, and a pair of leather-and-chrome Poul Kjaerholm seats are placed on the far side of the square open-hearth fireplace to form a smaller, more intimate conversation area.

The walls of this room are no less interesting. Amongst the artefacts are a painting by Sonia Delaunay and a glass arrangement of bow, spears and arrows by Swedish glass designer Eva Englund.

On the far side of this hallway there is a smaller family sitting area with a TV and music system, and beyond that is their son's bedroom. Their daughter, who is now at university, has a self-contained flat on the far side of the living room, with a separate outside entrance.

Back in the main living room, steps go down from the kitchen-breakfast level to a lower ground-floor bedroom, bathroom and another sitting room with large sliding glass

doors that open out onto the deck and lakeside. This lower-level master bedroom has two unusual Arne Jacobsen chairs with arms, and on the shelf above the bed there are three contemporary silver candlesticks by British designer Matthew Hilton. Beside the bed is another well-established classic, an Eileen Gray table in chrome and glass and on it a cylindrical light, one of the modern designs produced by the Edholms company, Mect.

The Edholms' house was built in a modern style and features large open spaces with panel windows which provide an almost neutral base in which to display their collection of modern classic furniture. This house is not a museum or showcase—its primary function is as a family home—but it combines the two with ease because of a good allocation of space and simple background decoration and design.

LEFT: Unusual Arne Jacobsen chairs with arms sit in front of the vertical blinds of the lower ground-floor main bedroom. Beyond the blinds is the deck area that the Edholms added so that they could enjoy seasonal outdoor living.

ABOVE: The casual dining area is to the left of the kitchen on the lower level of the main living room. The Miro-like painting on the wall was done for an advertising project.

LEFT: The upper-level bedroom ceiling is curved. It forms part of the graceful overhanging roof that can be seen beyond the sliding windows, opening out over the lush, green, jungle-like woods beyond.

RIGHT: The lower ground-floor utility space contains the shower room with cement walls and a simple gully recess in the floor to drain away the water. Wind that travels through it from the open sides of the structure dries the surfaces naturally.

tree-top territory

Ken Israel was an advertising designer in Sydney, Australia, when he decided to radically change his lifestyle and build his own home on an overgrown hillside outside the city. He designed an environmentally friendly wooden home with open-0panel sides that give access to the elements. It is his Eden, a place where he can relax and forget city life.

ABOVE: From beside the dining table, stairs lead up to the bedroom and past one of the many open windows. The internal walls and built-in fittings are made from Victorian ash and flooded gumwood.

RIGHT: The kitchen and dining area of the living space on the main floor opens out onto the wooden deck outside. Fixtures and fittings are simple but adequate.

The setting of Ken Israel's home is very important because the outdoors is visible from every room in the house. It was designed to be in harmony with the location and the natural elements that surround it.

The raised, timber-framed structure was designed with the help of architect Peter Stutchbury, who had studied the design of the homes of the indigenous peoples of New Guinea and Australia. These peoples believe that a building should put as little pressure on the earth as possible, so only stilt-like supports and a small cement wall connect Ken's house and the ground. Ken himself worked alongside a team of builders to clear the site.

The three-storey house lies at the bottom of a steep hill. There is no formal path and the final leg of the journey to the front door is over a two-plank wooden bridge that crosses a plant-filled gorge. The bridge finishes on a wooden platform from which you enter the main living room.

The small galley-style kitchen is situated at the rear of this room. A long table and folding wooden seats occupy the centre, and when the window panels in the side walls are pushed back it feels like the venue for a camp-site feast or picnic. Shelves stretching across the back wall hold simple ceramic and wooden bowls and hand-thrown pottery plates. A refrigerator, the electric bedside light upstairs and the washing machine on the floor below are among the few electrical gadgets Ken allows in his home. The rest are kept in a hut that also serves as his office at the top of the hill near the main entrance to the plot because he wants to keep the amount of electrical radiation and current to a minimum.

Stairs on the lefthand side of the room lead to the upper storey of the house which is contained under a sail-like roof that overhangs the building on each side. Three of the walls consist of large sliding-glass panels which can be pushed right back to open the room to the elements. The fourth wall is more solid and is mainly constructed from wood.

In the back wall are a series of sliding wooden panels that conceal a small cabin bedroom for visitors, storage space for clothes and books and a separate lavatory and basin. In the outer wall of the lavatory enclosure a small pivoting wooden panel at head height allows the jungle-like forest view to be contemplated during ablutions. The rest of the main bedroom is simply furnished with an unbleached cotton futon on a raised wooden base, a hammock hung from the roof and a chair which Ken made out of driftwood and rope. Sometimes in the summer Ken abandons this more conventional bedroom and sleeps under canvas on the platform outside the front door. Here he listens, until he falls asleep, to the sounds of the lapping water in the bay and the swaying branches of the trees.

The internal walls of the building are made from light-coloured Victorian ash and pink-coloured flooded gumwood, but with time the differing colours have gradually mellowed to the same golden hue. The wooden interior is not only warm and attractive, it is also easy to maintain, needing only to be washed down from time to time. Outside, the walls are finished in hardy tallow wood.

On the bottom level of the house, reached by an external ladder-like stairway and set amongst tree ferns and boulders, is a utility room with a walk-in shower. This no-frills bathroom is elementary and unembellished but, like the kitchen, does everything it is supposed to.

This tree-top house is small and simple, but Ken says it feels right for him. It is unpretentious and natural, and its spartan interiors and lack of clutter are calming, as is the ever-changing natural decoration framed by the large windows.

family-friendly

Wayne and Gerardine Hemingway founded the fashion company Red or Dead and are credited with, among other things, making Dr Marten's shoes fashionable. Gerardine's first architectural project was designing the family's modern and functional 8,000-square-foot (730-square-metre) home. The layout accommodates the daily life of the couple's four children as well as providing ample storage space.

LEFT: The open-plan top floor has a rubberized climbing wall with raised foot- and hand-holds and a Ping-Pong table at one end. In the foreground is one of the pair of sofas made from the remains of the family's boat wrecked in a gale.

BELOW: A long line of built-in cupboards with brightly coloured laminate doors runs under the windows at the front of the house. The half-height walls of the corner kitchen have been painted with blackboard paint so that the children can draw on them.

Wayne and Gerardine Hemingway and their growing family enjoyed the space and countryside of West Sussex and decided to make it their home. They bought a property near Chichester, a Spanish hacienda-style building with numerous porticoes, but Gerardine knew it would never work for them as a family home

The Spanish house was demolished and on the levelled site Gerardine, who was responsible for designing the interiors of the Red or Dead shops, has created an efficient modern house, tailored to suit everyone's needs.

The result is a large open-plan family room with snooker and Ping-Pong tables, a climbing wall and a kitchen. The dining area is focused around a long sideboard designed by Gerardine and faced with cherrywood and brushed-steel-effect Formica. It is between the staircase leading to the lower floor and an ample sitting area arranged around the fireplace.

The length of the wall to the front of the house is filled with brightly coloured cupboards, faced in various shades of wipe-clean laminate and opened with practical linear handles. Inside are the toys, paperwork, files and general household junk that would otherwise clutter up the surfaces. With a large family to look after, Gerardine was well aware of the need to provide ample storage space. She decided that, where possible, furniture should be built in. Throughout the house most of the cupboards, some of the beds and all the wardrobes are purpose-built and fixed to the walls, saving floor space and creating a unity and basic style throughout the various rooms.

The twenty-foot-high ceiling in the living room and the muted colours of the walls make it light and spacious, but splashes of brighter colour and some unusual pieces of furniture prevent it from seeming empty or cold. The unusual furniture includes two long, deep sofas that have been constructed from the remains of the family's boat which was

RIGHT: The adult lounging space on the ground floor also doubles as an extra bedroom. The soft, restful colours make it an ideal place to unwind, and the view from the French doors opposite the bench seats is of the tree-filled garden beyond.

FAR RIGHT: The dining area with its long table and seating for ten features a sideboard designed by Gerardine and faced with coloured and steel-effect laminate. Behind the sideboard, stairs lead down to the lower rooms.

wrecked in a gale. The Hemingways had the broken bow removed and the remains of the hull halved and set on frames, then seat and back cushions were made to fit. Two other chairs made from rope and wood continue this nautical feel. These serviceable pieces work well with the rubber climbing surface that spreads over half the wall at the far end of the room and the Ping-Pong table in front. Nothing is child-free in this room; it is an inclusive family space.

The corner kitchen, at the dining area end of the room, has been designed so that whoever is cooking can keep an eye on the children. The two lower sections of the half-height wall that encloses the space are painted with blackboard paint, one for a shopping list and the other a drawing board.

The wall of south-facing windows overlooks the tree tops and the eight acre (seven hectare) garden below, and allows the adults to supervise the children at play. Heating pipes were laid into the concrete floor, which means that there is constant warmth but the floors are easy to clean. The walls are also concrete but have been painted with washes of colour, which gives them a softer appearance.

On the ground floor behind the staircase is a 'utility' section, consisting of a cloakroom, boot storage, laundry room and nanny's room. At the bottom of the staircase is a small sitting room for the adults, with two long banquettes covered in fake fur that can be rearranged into a double bed.

Behind this room a corridor leads to the bedrooms and bathrooms. The first room on the right is the couple's eldest son's room, with a curved glass brick wall and a wardrobe designed by Gerardine and painted in metallic blue car paint. The other furniture, which includes a 1970s bedside light and a 1960s white chair and table, was chosen by their son. Next along the corridor is a small bathroom and their youngest son's room. Opposite is Wayne and Gerardine's bedroom with an en-suite bathroom. The wall from the door to the windows is covered with built-in wardrobes with coloured laminate facades. The room has two walls of glass, one overlooking the garden and the other leading out onto a deck area. Set back to the other side of the deck are the girls' bedrooms.

Although this house has been designed practically, its modern style and approach has not been sacrificed.

The Pearce family home has been built in stages and is almost biographical, as its development charts the changes in Stephen's life. The central core, a square, well-proportioned house with Gothic-style arched windows and elements of Georgian design, was erected in 1937. The house is comfortable and traditional in its layout. The two-level sitting room with a wooden balcony doubles as a corridor at the upper edge of the double-height main room. A large, vernacular-style fireplace and chimney breast with a step-fronted facade dominate the room and the fire radiates enough heat to fill both levels of the tall space.

Well-upholstered armchairs and sofas with plain cream-coloured loose covers are arranged in front of the hearth. In the winter evenings the warm glow of the embers is enhanced by the mellow light reflected from wall sconces, made by Pearce from polished brass discs, and wrought-iron candle holders hung on the whitewashed walls.

Off the sitting room is a compact square kitchen with handmade wooden cupboards that have pivoting panel doors on the upper units. There is plenty of storage space, much of it filled with the distinctive terra-cotta and white pottery made at Pearce's Shanagarry Pottery.

Upstairs in the main house, reached by the balcony, is the spacious main bedroom and bathroom. The sliding doors of the wardrobe in this room are decorated with painted gold- and silver-leaf panels by Pearce's godfather, the architect and artist Patrick Scott. The tall windows here and in the living room are curtained with thick, woollen, blue-and-cream-check Kerry horse blankets looped back to the window frame with bridle-like leather bands.

When Stephen became a father he built a tall tower-like addition to the house connected to the front of the main

irish oriental

ABOVE: The fireplace and stepped chimney breast in the double-height sitting room of the original house. Through the doorway is the kitchen, which is linked by the conservatory to the tower.

RIGHT: Next to the round fireplace is one of Patrick Scott's metallic-leafed paintings on the only solid wall of the Tea House. Even in the winter this room is warm because of underfloor heating.

A potter of international repute, Stephen Pearce has many other interests. He travelled extensively before returning home to the family pottery and the village of Shanagarry outside Cork on the south coast of Ireland. Here he designed and built much of his own home, which has grown to accommodate family demands. The design of the house incorporates an unusual blend of Irish and oriental styles.

RIGHT: The Orientally inspired Tea House has a wonderful view of Ballycotton Bay.

house by a corridor. The doorway between the two buildings is rounded at the top and bottom as a result of a trip to Morocco where he was inspired by similar-shaped doorways. The tower contains a play area, bathroom and bedrooms.

Later Pearce added a conservatory linking the back of the tower to the side of the main house, opening up what had been the kitchen's outside wall. Underfloor heating means that the fired-clay tiles, used in the conservatory and throughout the ground floor, are always comfortable to walk on in socks or bare feet. The heat also helps the plants in the conservatory to thrive in its warm, light atmosphere.

Along one wall of the conservatory is a modern console table with a complex wire-grid base that was originally part of a shop display in the Issey Miyake shop in London. Stephen says he annoyed the shop manager for months until he allowed him to buy it. The table is now covered with handmade wooden bowls created by Ciaran Forbes, a monk and master woodturner at Glenstore Abbey.

As the family grew, another annex was added on the far side of the house, at the opposite end from the tower, and at around the same time Stephen started the construction of the Tea House. This Oriental-inspired construction was built on a plot of land at the end of the garden, through a small copse of trees that he planted when he was ten years old in what was then the grounds of his parents' home.

The Tea House has a thatched roof and mainly glass walls, which give a 180-degree view of the marshland and watery landscape of Ballycotton Bay beyond. Ballycotton Bay is one of the three most important landing sites for migratory birds in Europe, so many rare and unusual birds can often be spotted from its cosy confines. There is a prevailing feeling of tranquillity and calm here, and again underfloor heating means that it is snug and comfortable even on a cold day.

On the wooden floor of the Tea House, futons and thick cushions can be arranged for sitting or reclining, and a circular fireplace, with a rounded brick hearth, has been cut into an angular chimney breast. A painting hanging on the wall beside the fire is also by Patrick Scott, and the metallic disc in its centre echoes the shape of the unusual round fireplace. It was Scott's encouragement that developed Stephen's interest in architecture, so you could almost say that the artistic cycle is complete.

Although the Pearce home has been built a bit at a time and the styles vary from classic Georgian to Oriental minimalism, the interiors are unified by plain white walls, unfussy furniture and well-placed objects. With an eye for shape and detail, Stephen has brought together the diverse elements of his home.

FAR LEFT: The spacious 'Ballroom' cottage is
furnished with a mix of old and contemporary
furniture placed in a pale setting. A mini-kitchen is
concealed in the painted armoire against the
back wall.

LEFT: The terra-cotta walls of the middle room in the
first cottage provide a perfect backdrop for a series
of black-and-white prints depicting the letters of
the alphabet.

at home in the hamptons

Todd Hase is one of the new and important names in furniture design in America, and his classic pieces are found in the homes of Cameron Diaz, Kevin Spacey and Bruce Willis. Hase and his wife Amy take regular breaks from their busy Manhattan lives to spend weekends at their Hamptons home, created out of two renovated 1940s cottages.

The Hases' weekend home, on the edge of an eleven-acre (four-and-a-half hectare) wooded plot, is designed to function like a chameleon. The rooms are dual-purpose: during the day they present classic, chic settings but at night they are transformed into luxurious bedrooms for family and guests. The colours that have been used are rich and sumptuous, brightened by practical, pale-washed wood floors and light from newly installed French windows.

Unlike many New Yorkers with homes in the Hamptons, the Hases use their retreat all year round rather than only during the summer, so the furnishings and decor are designed to work in all weathers. By the time the family arrives at the cottages on Friday evenings, their young daughters are ready to be lifted into their beds, but on entering the cottages it is difficult to see exactly where the beds are.

Glass-panelled double front doors open from the terrace directly into the sitting room of the first cottage. This room is decorated in a relaxing muted-green scheme with two sofas, one an eighteenth-century Oriental carved platform and the other an upholstered mohair velvet piece of Todd's design. The former makes up into an ample double bed for guests. The fireplace mantel, dated 1720, is local to the Hamptons although, to the right, the antique Oriental spirit house raised on a modern Perspex display plinth has travelled from much further afield.

The second room, reached by another set of double doors, has rich brick-red painted walls and a sofa under the window. The window is dressed with a fine linen inner curtain and outer ones of suede. Against the rich colour of the walls a framed collection of black-and-white photographs by Igor Vishnyakov depicts images representing the letters of the alphabet. One of Todd's oval coffee tables in macassar ebony sits in front of the sofa. His designs are modern but with historical references, which is not so surprising when you discover that he was born into a family of antiques dealers. The sofa in this room also becomes a single bed.

The blend of old and new, which is such an influence in Todd's work, can be seen in the sunny yellow end room where at last you find a recognizable bed. This grand piece of furniture is based on drawings of Marie-Antoinette's bed. Beside it, at its foot, are small tables designed by Todd.

Although this is a family home, the couple wanted to retain some sense of grandeur, and they felt that with small cottages it was important to use colour to make each room individual and special. Yet the finishes are practical and the narrow-plank lime-washed floors throughout are easy to sweep clean.

The Hases wanted the second cottage, jokingly called 'The Ballroom', to be dramatically different. They took out most of the internal walls and opened it up to a high-vaulted ceiling, then put French doors in place of all the original windows. The furniture in this cottage can all be pushed back to the walls to make a big open space where the children play or where dances and family parties can be held. A dozen gilt ballroom-style chairs are placed around the walls, so there is plenty of seating when entertaining.

The 'Ballroom' is furnished with antique and modern pieces. Sycamore coffee and side tables, mirrors and sofas from 'the family business' mix with antique needlepoint-upholstered chairs, a French chandelier, a painted armoire and a large daybed which makes a comfortable double, with two foldaway beds stored underneath for the girls.

Each cottage has a bathroom, and there are also two kitchen areas. Off the red room in the first cottage is a well-equipped kitchen with full-size refrigerator, oven, range and sink, but in the second cottage the cooking facilities are disguised behind the ornate doors of the armoire. Inside is a miniature but complete kitchen.

The Hase family's weekend home has got the laid-back lifestyle down to a fine art. Space may be restricted, but they have gone full-out for style and splendour, and with clever planning they accommodate day and overnight entertaining.

ABOVE: The eighteenth-century carved Chinese platform in the main room of the first cottage can be transformed into a comfortable double bed at night. The fire surround is local and dates from 1720.

RIGHT: In the third room of the first cottage is a bed modelled on drawings of a bed owned by Queen Marie-Antoinette of France. A modern chair and table, designed by Todd, provide a sitting area beyond the footboard.

colourful

PREVIOUS PAGES: Tony Baratta's dining and
sitting room in Long Island is decorated with
white walls and vivid splashes of colour.

LEFT: David Champion's small kitchen is
dramatically decorated in black and white with
ethnic artefacts displayed on open shelves.

FAR LEFT: Opposite the foot of the bed is the 'BG'
sofa. Canvas curtains hide the bookcases during the
day, and cover the door and windows at night.

bohemian bedsit

David Champion is a designer and decorator with a high-profile international client list. He also owns a shop selling an eclectic mix of ethnic and modern design in the fashionable Westbourne Grove area of London. This blend of styles has also been used to decorate his pied-à-terre, and what this residence lacks in space it makes up for in impact with dramatic colours and luxurious materials.

David Champion's seventh floor, three-room flat is at the top of a 1930s apartment block near Notting Hill in west London. Although the apartment is of modest proportions (the bathroom and kitchen are tiny and only the main room could be described as a real room), David chose to ignore the perceived wisdom of using pale colours to make a space appear larger. Instead he opted for maximum impact.

The main room has to contend with the challenge of combining sleeping and living facilities, so the layout was critical. The main feature is the bed, placed in the centre of the room against the internal wall and facing the windows. Between the foot of the bed and the sitting area is a low table which places some distance between the two parts of the room. A long three-seater sofa has its back to the window, and a gap behind it forms a small passageway which gives access to the books that are stacked on shelves on either side of and over the windows.

Pieces of furniture designed by David include the long leather sofa, christened 'BG' after Barbara Golan, the fifties model he says he can imagine perched on the upholstered leather arm. He describes the shape as basically Regency but with more shapely lines and blond wooden legs. The black-and-white 'Vogue' dining chairs resting against the walls are his generous-sized answer to the meaner, leaner version of upholstered dining chair found in the high street shops.

Although the sofa and chairs take up a portion of the room, it is the bed that dominates. On top of a black-and-gold quilt cover lies an orange-velvet-and-gold throw from the Lebanon. Bronze-striped and tufted pillows contribute to the regal air. The narrow table at the foot of the bed is covered with canvas gilded with gold leaf and is used as a desk, dining table and hideaway for the TV, which sits beneath the regal cover. It also notionally divides the sleeping and the sitting areas.

The recess behind the bedhead is lined with cream-and-brown striped canvas, which David describes as a modest material, but one that in his hands looks sophisticated. Running the whole length of the walls above the bed is a

FAR LEFT: Behind the bedhead, cream canvas curtains conceal rows of shelves and hanging rails for clothes. At the foot of the bed a low table disguises the TV and doubles as a dining and coffee table.

LEFT: On the lilac-grey walls of the main room there is a gallery-like arrangement of paintings by South African artist Nicolaas Maritz. By using similar frames David has made the collection appear a unified rather than disparate mix.

chrome pole from which cream canvas curtains, bordered with brown, are hung by chrome eyelets. These are arranged so that when they are pulled back the stripes stack in neat vertical lines. The curtains conceal the hanging and shelf space of the wardrobe but create a plain wall when pulled across.

Opposite the bed, a similar arrangement conceals bookcases on either side of the original windows and door, which lead on to a small terrace overlooking the busy street below. When the curtains are drawn over the door and windows at night, the well-stocked bookcases are revealed.

When David moved into his gem of an apartment the floor was painted black and the ceiling white, but he felt it would work better the other way round, so he painted the ceiling black and put a pale covering on the floor. The walls are a lilac-grey colour and covered, like a gallery, with the paintings of fellow South African Nicolaas Maritz.

The works feature stylized outlines of Cape Town's Table Mountain, vessels, vases and tugboats and have been collected by Champion. The ceramics of another South African artist, Hylton Nel, are also to be found in the bathroom and kitchen.

The monotone theme of the main room is continued in the bathroom and kitchen. The kitchen has a row of black-painted shelves above a splashback of black-and-white checkerboard ceramic tiles. Black-painted units are topped with slabs of marble, and a small electric stove, refrigerator and sink are neatly arranged amongst them.

Hung on the black-gloss-painted wall of the bathroom are African hats and drawings depicting hairstyles from an African barber's shop. Dotted sporadically amongst the white ceramic tiles of the splashback are single black tiles, and the sides of the white ceramic bath and basin are also painted black.

David Champion's pied-à-terre is a perfect example of how small can be beautiful. Although the space may be confined, style need know no bounds. It is also an example of how rules can be broken. By ignoring the age-old advice of using pale walls and few artefacts in small areas, he has created an interest-filled, colour-packed bijou residence.

LEFT: A pair of matching Regency-style sofas stands against the wall under two wall-bracket lights and a chandelier covered in opulent crystal drops. The height of the wall is accentuated by a large painting of two women in period dress.

RIGHT: The dining area of the grand salon is furnished with a 1940s white metal table and chairs by Rene Prou. The fine structure of the furniture is echoed in the modern chandelier by Dominic Bernard.

designer digs

Chantal Thomass is a successful fashion designer whose label is found on some of Europe's most delicate lingerie and hosiery. Her home, a spacious third floor apartment in a turn-of-the-century building in central Paris has grand style and is decorated with light, fancy and feminine decor that epitomizes her womanly ways.

The decoration of the large period rooms of Chantal Thomass's apartment has an unashamedly and distinctly feminine feel, with pastel colours and delicate tulle, toile and appliqué floral motifs on curtains and cushions. Even the furniture is highly decorative and whimsical. Finding a suitable setting was important so that these unusual furnishings could be arranged to their best advantage. 'It took a while to find the right place,' explains Chantal, 'but what appealed to me about this apartment was the large rooms and the fact that the original marble bathrooms were in good condition. The only room that had to be totally redone was the kitchen.'

From the entrance hall you step into a sizeable room. At one end is the dining area with a white metal 1940s table and chairs by Rene Prou. The twig-like plaster candlestick on the table and the many-branched chandelier above are by a contemporary designer, Dominic Bernard. On the table a set of glasses, at the front revealing ladies in period costume but when turned showing the ladies in the nude, were a present from a friend who found them in a flea market.

At the other end of the room is what Chantal refers to as the salon and library. The walls on either side of the pink-grey marble fireplace are filled with shelves, the supports of which are carved ornate brackets, painted off-white with gold detailing. On the wall between two large windows hangs a predominately red painting, one of a pair of designs for an embroidery. The other is in the passageway above a console table. Beneath the picture that hangs between the salon and the dining areas is a long chest of drawers covered by Chantal in decoupage using pictures from old magazines. She collects fashion magazines, both old and new.

In front of a pair of candy-coloured two-seater sofas are a couple of small tables shaped like a spade and a heart from

LEFT: Two side tables in the sitting area of the main room were bought second hand and repainted gold and white to complement the overall scheme of the room. The decorative wooden floor is original to the apartment.

ABOVE: The dressing room is decorated with pink-and-white 'Brigitte Bardot' gingham. Part of Chantal's collection of shoes can be seen on top of a cabinet in the foreground.

a pack of playing cards. They were a dark, unattractive colour when she bought them so she employed a decorator to paint them white and gold so that they were more in keeping with the rest of the room.

In Paris, buildings of this age tend to have generous-sized reception rooms but tiny bedrooms hidden away down a corridor. But Chantal's own bedroom is a good size and decorated in a creamy off-white, grey and soft pink. At the large window the curtains are of grey taffeta decorated with appliquéd flowers cut from an old dress found by Chantal in a flea market. Beyond her bedroom is one of the two bathrooms with its original marble frieze and large ceramic handbasin.

On the other side is her dressing room, lined with what she refers to as 'Brigitte Bardot' pink-and-white gingham. The walls are filled with rails of clothes, but most are never worn; they are from her past designer collections and old or antique clothes that she has bought. The clothes that she actually wears take up a tiny part of the room. As well as collecting clothes and shoes, Chantal also has a group of small figures dressed in period costumes, all made from shells.

The hallway that leads from the bedrooms and bathrooms to the main rooms is lined with cupboards along one side. These have been softened and made more decorative with panels of old material, originally a mattress cover, once again one of her finds from a market.

The kitchen, which was completely gutted and replaced, is also a family room and is where most meals are eaten. The dining area is used mostly for formal entertaining. A professional-style range is surrounded by handpainted cabinets specially made for her by a couple of furniture makers. The cupboards were decorated with a soft paint effect which Chantal describes as essentially a country look placed in the context of the city.

Feminine and *stylish* are the words that best describe this Parisian apartment, and it is a look that comes naturally to the fashion designer who lives here. From the pink-and-white 'Bardot' gingham curtains pinned up in gathers in the dressing room to the glass pendants and twig-like branches of the chandeliers, each space has been thoughtfully and carefully dressed.

oriental overtones

Peter Ting is an acclaimed ceramics designer who has been commissioned by the British royal family. The decoration of his 1930s south London home combines two opposing styles: traditional elements from his Hong Kong childhood and a clean-cut contemporary look more readily associated with a man whose work is at the cutting edge of modern design.

LEFT: The contemporary bedroom area has a colourful two-sided fireplace which makes a significant impact in the otherwise low-key scheme.

ABOVE: The angular lines of the doorways and opening of the adjacent ground-floor rooms makes this limited space seem taller and more spacious.

ABOVE: The ornate double doors lead from the chinoiserie dining room to the modern hallway beyond. Decorative panels have been placed at the top, making the doors appear taller.

RIGHT: The walls of the 'mock' Oriental dining room are covered with brown paper above the faux rail and panelled in silk below it. The black-framed pictures contain paper cutouts from a supermarket in London's Soho.

The bathroom is enclosed off one corner of the room and a small lavatory and handbasin are housed in a cupboard-style space off the turn of the staircase. All is calm and well ordered but the space avoids monotony with flashes of colour in soft furnishings and panels. One panel is a narrow inset of artwork by Peter's close friend, Irish artist Brian Kennedy, which forms a continuous and gradually changing band of colour across the front of the wall of white cupboard doors.

To discover Peter's more traditional Oriental influence you have to go back downstairs, where double doors, almost indistinguishable from the wall, open into the dining room. The room has been created from a diverse array of items which took years to accumulate. The dining table, matching sideboard, chairs and two small consoles were bought from a second-hand shop in Cheshire. Peter discovered later that the shipment had come from Fukien near Shanghai, his mother's home town. In the bay window is a silk-covered daybed scattered with richly coloured and lavishly embroidered cushions, but not all the furnishings have such a special provenance. The silk tassels were bought from Chinatown in San Francisco, and the fake jade and carved cinnabar discs and beads on the tassels came from China Town in London's Soho and from shops in Manchester's Chinese district.

The wall opposite the double doors is covered with a block of framed silk and paper filigree images, concocted from ordinary frames with offcuts of silk and spray-mounted paper cutouts. The picture rail is made of glued Petersham tape. A pair of cuffs from theatrical costumes for the Peking Opera are fixed over two plastic light shades by means of Velcro strips and embellished with a few extra tassels. The elaborate light fixture is from a do-it-yourself plastic flatpack kit which originally had bright red-and-green panels, but the colour was washed off and panels of fine silk added. Although the colour of the walls is rich and adds to the feeling of intimacy, they are in fact covered with cheap brown wrapping paper.

The centrepiece of the room is the table generously set with oversized Riedel wine glasses and grand, printed decoupage plates by American designer Scott Potter. Bowls by French florist Christian Tortu sit in the centre, but the *pièce-de-résistance* is a prototype of Ting's contemporary, minimal but multi-functional bone china spinning dishes. Another of his works, a highly ornate china cone, placed inside a glass dome, and modelled on Victorian aspic moulds, sits on a side table under one of a pair of calligraphy panels.

Peter Ting's work and home indulge in two styles, and the result is an unusual dwelling. Although there are carefully measured doses of colour, Peter saved most of it to make one grand dramatic gesture in his opulent dining room.

As Peter Ting explains, 'I love open minimal space, but also the ornateness and colour of chinoiserie. My family are from Hong Kong so that traditional opulence and decorative style is very much part of me.' To accommodate both passions, he has converted his semi-detached house into a home with two very distinct appearances. The transformation took more than five years.

The entrance hall is plain and white, and leads through to the back of the house where the doorways have been knocked out and replaced with simple angular openings. To one side is a white-painted TV room, on the other a simple modern kitchen with richly coloured wooden accessories. From the hall a white-walled staircase leads to the upper level and what was once three separate rooms. This is now a single open-plan space with a bed area and sitting section. The longest wall is covered with cupboards that conceal a home office, a 'treasure' cupboard filled with pottery, glass and artefacts, others for clothing and a fold-out work desk.

spiritual home

Nitish Bharadwaj, a Bollywood actor, director and former politician and his wife Monisha, a classical dancer, author and documentary producer, live with their children in a 1930s apartment in Breach Candy on the outskirts of Mumbai. Its decoration has been influenced by the Hindu philosophy of Vastu, which places importance on the balance of the elements.

The Bharadwajs' home, on the upper floor of an apartment block, is cool and relaxing, and has been decorated and arranged according to the principles of the Hindu doctrine of Vastu Shanti. These are designed to 'invoke the blessings of the celestial elements' and share many basic themes with Feng Shui. The philosophy works around the five elements of nature – air, water, fire, earth and space, and the ideal of achieving harmony.

When Nitish and Monisha first viewed the apartment they were undecided about it. The floors were covered in thick plastic matting and a low false ceiling had been installed. But they peeled back a corner of the matting and found the original 1930s decorative floor tiles and their structural engineer revealed that beams and pillars were hidden behind layers of decoration. These discoveries convinced them to buy the flat, and after six months of restoration work they moved in.

The Vastu balance of the elements is an important part of a Hindu household. Air and the flow of it is aided by air-conditioning units and large ceiling fans. Tall windows in each room are protected by decorative grilles but open to bring in light and air. Water is represented in the main bedroom by a wall of sea-blue paint, which reminds Nitish and Monisha that the sea is just a few metres away. Fire can be represented by colour but is actually seen here flickering in a lamp that burns at a small shrine in the sitting area. There are also splashes of fire colours, such as the gold on the raw silk bolster covers in the bay window seat and the gilding on the Tanjore pictures painted on glass.

Earth is present in pots of herbs, and the furniture is carefully positioned so that there is a maximum amount of uninterrupted floor space. Two of the doors from the main room have glass panels, which also add to the flow of light

LEFT: In front of the curved window seat in the family sitting area of the main living room, a low table supports a selection of old betel-nut cutters. The colourful original encaustic-tiled floor has been carefully restored.

LEFT: The blue wall in the main bedroom represents the element of water. On the floor are some of the original star-patterned floor tiles that were found under layers of matting.

RIGHT: The rich red wall in the guest bedroom complements the darker shades of the handmade bed quilt, which was made according to a traditional American design by a local quilting expert.

and the feeling of roominess. The panels contain etched glass depicting Lord Shiva as the god of dance Nataraja, particularly appropriate to Monisha's dancing background.

The layout of the apartment is J-shaped. The main room which forms the back of the letter is divided into a formal seating area, a dining section and a family space which centres around the bay window. The formal seating area is arranged around a glass-topped table with ornate wrought-iron legs. Each of the chairs and the two sofas are decorated with a different patterned fabric.

The wall between the dining section and the family sitting area was partially knocked down to aid the flow of air and light. In the curved bay window behind the low wall is a fitted seat with colourful cushions and on a low table is a collection of antique betel-nut cutters. There is also a statue of Vishnu in a recess by the door to the children's room.

The toe of the J is the children's bedroom and bathroom, and to the right of the cap of the J is Nitish and Monisha's

bedroom and bathroom. Opposite their room is a guest bedroom, a bathroom and a tiny kitchen which overlooks the main road. The main bedroom with its blue wall is simply furnished with a wrought-iron bed and a wall of wardrobes lined with airtight metal cabinets, which are essential to keep clothes from becoming mouldy during the monsoon.

The guest bedroom has a deep-magenta painted wall, and a more Western feel, mainly because of the quilt made by Geeta Khandelwal, a Bombay-based award-winning quilt maker who used Indian textiles to make the quilt but followed a traditional American design. The pink-and-red prints are amplified by the strength of the colour on the wall.

Although the principles of Vastu have a spiritual basis, they provide elementary but useful guidelines to decorating a home, and in the Bharadwajs' home the result is harmonious. The elements are all present but not dominant, and the original features of the house contribute a mix of both pattern and colour to the overall scheme.

RIGHT: The comfortable seating arrangement which lies between the 'Hang Out' room and the dining area and kitchen beyond is filled with well-upholstered traditional-style sofas. The mirror above the sofa reflects light and a view of the Manhattan skyline.

room at the top

Fashion designer Betsey Johnson is one of New York's original 'rock chicks'. She launched her own label in 1978 in partnership with Chantal Bacon, and numbers Courtney Love, Helena Bonham Carter and Minnie Driver as fans. Her home is a vibrantly colourful, whimsically decorated two-level apartment on the seventeenth floor of a building on Fifth Avenue.

Colour makes a bold statement as soon as you walk through the doors of Betsey Johnson's duplex apartment. The vibrant yellow walls came about because she saw the colour on the cover of a magazine and loved it, and she teamed it with purple because the colours are situated directly opposite each other on the colour wheel.

The yellow walls and purple floor are seen throughout the open-plan lower floor of the apartment, a space which was created by knocking two smaller apartments together and taking out the walls that had previously made up five small rooms. Also tackled during this building phase was the reconstruction of the glass-box room on the upper-level roof garden, which contains Betsey's seasonal bedroom.

Downstairs, to the left of the front door is Betsey's walk-in wardrobe, the walls of which are divided into rows and rows of shelves. Many are filled with neatly folded piles of T-shirts, cardigans and sweaters; others hold opaque plastic boxes with labels listing their contents.

Beyond the entrance and wardrobe is a substantial open space Betsey refers to as the 'Hang Out' room. The windows here, and throughout the apartment, are draped with a collection of antique piano shawls and vintage frocks on

coathangers, suspended from rails of plumber's copper piping. These window decorations have been bought from a wide range of junks shops, antiques fairs and markets, where she loves to shop.

Also in the 'Hang Out' space is a spare bed. 'I sleep upstairs in the spring and summer, but when it's cold I come down here', she explains. Behind the bed is the more intimate sitting and TV area with three sofas arranged in a U shape. Two of the sofas are upholstered and cushioned in a bright yellow floral fabric. In front of the sofas is Betsey's jewellery table with pots, jars and bowls overflowing with real and costume jewellery.

Behind the single non-floral sofa is a dining area with a mixture of vintage and contemporary furniture, dominated by a large-scale, colourful painting of parrots. She saw the painting when passing a second-hand shop and knew instinctively that it would be just the right thing for that space on her wall.

Next to the dining area, through another shawl-draped opening, is the equally colourful kitchen with a small round table and four chairs. A steel sink runs along one wall, with a work surface and cabinets on the facing wall.

Going back through the 'Hang Out' space, you pass a small, relatively calm corner with a 1950s boudoir chair with integral mirror near the doorway to the bathroom. The internal glass-brick wall of the bathroom is shaded with more piano shawls and inside, the purple-painted walls are covered with sparkling clear-glass tiles. A roll-top bath is surrounded by pink floral curtains, and a row of glittering vintage party shoes line up under a chrome stand with shelves of perfume bottles and trinkets. Also in this room is a graceful old porcelain handbasin with an integral area of useful surface on either side and legs that look as though they came from a piece of period furniture.

Open-tread stairs lead from outside the bathroom to the roof garden and the now stable glass box, above, which contains Betsey's bedroom. The one-and-a-half solid walls of this space are covered in a green version of the floral print used for the sofa upholstery downstairs, and the remaining glass walls are partially concealed by more rows of fine voile and lace dresses. Her ornate iron bedstead lies beneath a glittering chandelier and on the far side of the stair opening there is a small handbasin and an antique cabinet.

Betsey's passionate love of colour and vintage materials has had a significant impact and effect on the interior of her lofty home, and although there are those who say less is more, in her fabulously decorative world only more and more will do. In this New York apartment colour rules.

LEFT: Open-tread stairs on the left lead up to Betsey's seasonal bedroom. The double doors on the far side of the pillar contain her walk-in wardrobe. The space in the foreground is part of the 'Hang Out' area.

FAR RIGHT: The cold-weather bed in the corner of the 'Hang Out' space can be made more private by drawing together some of the numerous vintage piano shawls that are used as curtains and room dividers.

RIGHT: The purple-and-pink bathroom with clear glass tiles has a classic roll-top bath and a vintage ceramic handbasin. Pink shower curtains, printed with vintage-style blooms and lined with frilled pink muslin hangings, make the bath an eyecatching feature.

a stable place

Wendy Smyth and Richard Gibson's Belfast-based company specializes in high-quality men's and women's shirts, produced under their label Smyth & Gibson. Their home, a converted stable block on the outskirts of the city, has retained much of the simple structure of the agricultural building but uses modern free-standing walls and colour to divide up the large spaces and add warmth and interest.

Richard and Wendy's home is in the lush green country-side on the outskirts of Belfast, but just ten minutes by car from their shop in the city centre and twenty minutes' drive from Richard's office. This perfect location, and the opportunity to develop an old agricultural building into a modern home with an unusual aspect, was what drew them to this area.

Their hilltop home is a converted stable block, a single-storey building, dating from the 1860s, in the shape of an oblong with a missing section on the right side. Through this narrow opening there is an uninterrupted view down to Belfast Lough. But the old stables were derelict when the couple bought them and they had to camp in a caravan in the grounds for six months until one section was made habitable.

Now the main living area is in the back of the complete, long side of the oblong. Here an inner frame was built to support the roof, which was raised above the level of the original brick walls, creating a gap infilled with glass panel windows. The newly laid concrete floor is warmed by underfloor heating and there is also a large fireplace.

The couple wanted to maintain the simplicity of the structure so added only two free-standing walls at either end of the room. One wall conceals part of the kitchen and the other contains the fireplace. The reverse side of the fireplace wall forms one side of a passageway to the spare bedroom and the wall is shelved with row upon row of books. When it came to choosing colours for these two walls, Wendy looked at books on historical houses and found that yellow, blue and red were popular colours, so decided to work on a contemporary variation of that theme. She selected a duck-egg blue for the front of the kitchen and a golden yellow for the wall at the other end.

Striking purple linen curtains hanging from high-tension steel cables, like yacht rigging, cover the long

LEFT: The main living space looks towards the wall that conceals the kitchen. The outside walls were raised by the addition of high-level windows, but the basic stable structure has remained the same.

RIGHT: A free-standing wall acts as a barrier between the kitchen and the rest of the living space. Small openings are used to display vases and objects, and a large one gives a view onto the activities beyond.

windows overlooking the inner courtyard. At the other side the small narrow windows are left bare as they overlook a high grassy bank. When they are drawn the curtains create another wall of solid colour.

The kitchen is steel and equipped with a semi-industrial stove and highly efficient stainless-steel worktops. These give the room a professional feel, yet an opening in the partition wall means that whoever is working in the kitchen is shielded but not cut off from the rest of the room.

On the opposite side of the room, a golden wall contains the fireplace, which is the focus of the sitting area. Behind this wall is a small passageway leading to a spare bedroom and bathroom. The bedroom is furnished with a suite of 1950s furniture exhibited at the first Belfast Ideal Home show after World War II. In this room the curtains are bright red, carrying on Wendy's theme of strong colours.

To the right of the golden wall, a corridor leads to Wendy's studio, which has the original double-opening stable doors and a large cutting table where she creates prototype shirt patterns. Next to the studio is the 'snug', where large leather sofas are positioned on either side of an Aga stove which radiates warmth.

Beyond this room the corridor continues past the bright white bathroom, with a narrow band of turquoise mosaic flooring around the edge of the bath. In the far right corner of the top of the oblong is an entrance hall with the stone flag floor that was part of the original stable.

In the final segment of this side is a spacious master bedroom with a wall of glass-fronted drawers that were once fittings in a haberdashery shop. The drawers are now filled with the couple's clothes but still retain the old price labels and descriptions pasted on the drawer fronts.

On the far side of the kitchen the remaining part of the building houses a utility room and a refurbished stable where Wendy keeps her horse. The courtyard that the building wraps round is now a pebble-strewn patio area. Where many horses once trotted out, Koi carp now leap in an oblong pond, and by doorways where stable lads groomed their thoroughbred charges, Wendy and Richard sit out with friends on summer evenings.

In their business Smyth and Gibson offer a custom-tailoring service to suit individual requirements, sending swatches of fabrics in particular colourways and patterns to fulfil a customer's needs, and in their home they have managed to tailor a setting that suits their lifestyle. The farmyard origins of the house have now been replaced by a colourful, contemporary take on country style, a look that is sophisticated but relaxed and in tune with rural life.

LEFT: Vibrant orange voile curtains in the main bedroom create a warm glow when the sun shines through them. The glass-fronted drawers are an antique shop fitting from an old draper's store in the city.

RIGHT: The second internal wall at the sitting end of the main living room contains the fireplace and display niches. On the reverse side there is a bookcase with shelves for CDs, books and magazines.

LEFT: The dining area in the new extension centres around the polished wooden table and chairs padded with knitted and printed silk cushions. The Gothic-style window is original to the chapel but was moved to this new location when the extension was built.

RIGHT: In the sitting room Georgina's ukulele rests on the back of an armchair covered in one of her company's richly coloured velvet prints. Decorative and festive illumination is provided by strands of fairy lights.

material girl

Georgina von Etzdorf's distinctive signature is found on many luxurious and innovative textile designs. Her home, a primitive Methodist chapel built in 1877, is not far from the Salisbury headquarters of the company she runs with business partners Martin Simcock and Jonathan Docherty. Her home is decorated in an individual and bohemian style that features many examples of the vibrant von Etzdorf designs.

RIGHT: The pink-painted sitting
room is on the ground floor of
the converted chapel. The main
door, once used by the
congregation, is now covered by
a rug that Georgina designed,
and another lies on the floor.

LEFT: The main bathroom has
violet-and-turquoise-painted
tongue-and-groove panelling
and a roll-top bath.

The modern glass-panelled studios where Georgina and her colleagues design, develop and print their fabrics is a bicycle ride away, down leafy lanes, from the home she has lived in for more than fifteen years. The chapel, which is concealed from view by tall hedges, is on the outskirts of a small village.

Inside the converted chapel the sixteen-foot- (nearly five metres) high ceiling space was divided to provide two floors, and a small extension was added to the back. The extension now houses the spacious open-plan dining area with orange and green velvet curtains screening the French doors from the cottage-style garden beyond.

Wooden chairs, placed around the round French oak dining table, are padded seat and back with beautiful von Etzdorf printed velvet and fine knitted cushions. The chairs also double as coat racks with various scarves and fabric bags hanging from their backs.

The paint scheme on the walls of this room is curious. At the dining end of the room the walls are painted white, but the rest of the room which houses the kitchen is a vibrant sunny yellow. The two-tone effect was the result of experience. When Georgina went to buy the yellow paint, the man in the shop warned her against using it on all the walls because, he said, it would be too powerful. She ignored him and painted on, but found that four bright yellow walls made the room close in, so she painted the far end white, which she now feels helps to define the different areas and their uses, and cools and lightens the effect of the yellow.

A large old Frigidaire refrigerator stands in the kitchen and is part of the exotic von Etzdorf family history. It was bought by her parents in New York, shipped to Peru when the family moved there and then back to England, and eventually to the chapel.

An antique stove, inherited *in situ* in the chapel, still works and sits in the corner of the dining space. The Gothic arched window by the dining table was moved from a side wall and put into the new wall of this extension. Through a matching window in the kitchen, just above the sink, there is a splendid view of the aptly named Rambling Rector rose which envelops most of the garden beyond.

A two-colour approach to paintwork, similar to that used in the kitchen, can also be seen in the vivid pink sitting room.

Three walls have been painted bright pink, and the fourth a softer, white-based tone of the same colour. Georgina says that she and her friends find this room relaxing, a place where they can unwind. The bending silver pipes of a new log-burning stove snake their way across the hot-pink wall and through the ceiling to the room above. Velvet upholstered armchairs and a chaise longue are covered in more von Etzdorf prints and a rug she designed hangs over the no longer used main door through which the congregation used to enter. These days, instead of the ringing tones of the organ, the music you are most likely to hear in the chapel is that of the ukulele, the instrument that Georgina has been learning for several years.

To the side of the pink living room is a spare bedroom and a cloakroom with a vintage Doulton ceramic basin and a shower. A second door opens into the lobby and stairwell which lead to the upper floor. The first floor landing and bedrooms in the eaves are unexpectedly bright because there are a number of skylights, unhindered by curtains, that allow light to flood in. Georgina's own bedroom not only has small windows in the outside wall but also a large skylight over her bed, allowing the sunlight to wake her each morning and the stars to see her off to sleep.

Along the upper corridor is the main bathroom decorated in a combination of parma violet and turquoise tongue-and-groove panelling, with an old fashioned roll-top bath. On a doorknob by the handbasin is a silvery tinsel crown with fake pearls and gems, and various pieces of antique pottery and glass bring sparkle to the brightly coloured room.

At the end of the corridor is another spare bedroom, with one wall taken up by a paper painting by Dieter Pietsch. More of his work is found on the walls in the kitchen. Although her home is light and airy, Georgina admits she has a tendency to clutter and many possessions. 'I hang on to things I love because they carry on giving me pleasure', she says.

Georgina's home is decorated with artistic flair, bringing together elements that many other people would not think or dare to combine. The original character of the old church has been little altered, but her choice of vibrant colours and interesting accessories has softened the hard edges and brought a new breath of offbeat style to the place.

house of glass

Seattle-based glass artist Dale Chihuly's work is 'spontaneous, fast and from the gut'. He is a widely recognized artist and in 2001 had a major exhibition at the Victoria and Albert Museum in London. Other commissions include a frieze for the Rainbow Room at Rockefeller Center and a series at the Louvre in Paris. His home, which includes his studio, is a showcase for some of his amazing kaleidoscopic glasswork.

RIGHT: A spiral metal staircase leads up to a narrow walkway, giving access to the main bedroom. The main window is divided into shelves displaying Chihuly glass art.

Chihuly's headquarters are at the 'constantly evolving', 25,000-square-foot (2,300 square metre) space on the rim of Lake Union, purchased in 1990 and converted, designed and decorated by the artist himself. The building, once a boathouse where wooden racing shells were fabricated, is now divided into work, studio and living areas.

The work area is dominated by the glass-blowing arena which includes a row of high-temperature kilns. Beyond is a corridor of offices and a work kitchen, from where a chipboard-panelled staircase leads up to Chihuly's private living quarters. At the top of the stairs and to the left is the Blue Room studio with its green Astroturf floor covering. Here trays of liquid acrylic paints are kept constantly ready, alongside the various mops and buckets that Chihuly uses to create his spontaneous artworks.

Directly in front of the stairs is the playroom for his son, Jackson, consisting of a fantasy space with an abundance of toys. Passing through this you reach the open-plan living, dining and cooking room. The L-shaped cooking section is dominated by a yellow enamel 1950s stove, and in the shorter leg of the L there is a recessed double-fronted fridge. In front of the stove is a long dining table strewn with books.

Behind the kitchen is a modest-sized bathroom and to the front of the multi-purpose living space is a cosy television and hi-fi section with armchairs and windows overlooking the lake. After the TV room is the library. Here the window side is divided into a display area with twenty-five niches, each holding a piece of Chihuly's glass. The two facing walls are sectioned, from top to bottom, with narrow display shelves on which sit hundreds, if not thousands, of books, without their covers. Hanging from the ceiling above is a collection of accordions. A metal spiral staircase leads to a

FAR LEFT: The long dining room, where rowing boats were once built, is filled by a table made from an 26-metre (88-foot) length of Douglas fir. Chihuly's amazing concoctions of colourful spun glass form chandeliers that add a frivolous and decadent touch to the otherwise sparse room.

LEFT: The walls of the guest dining, kitchen and bedroom area are clad with punched-metal panels, which give the room a cosy, warm, insulated feeling. The bed faces a window that looks out over the water, and is covered with one of Chihuly's vast collection of Navaho blankets.

narrow walkway which makes it practical to reach the upper levels of books and the main bedroom tucked into the eaves of the roof.

Whatever Chihuly does, it is with passion. His erratic but consuming form of commitment can be seen in his collections. He seldom has time to seek out and buy just one thing, so often purchases existing collections and adds them to his own. Along with an estimated 40,000 books and his art collection, there are shelves full of Native American blankets, an enviable collection of Edwin Curtis sepia gravure prints, ceramic cowboy and Indian figures, old motorbikes and papier-mâché masks, but somehow all are ordered, arranged and unduplicated.

Below his living quarters, at lake level, is the Navaho Room where the blankets, baskets and motorbikes are displayed. In the centre there is a huge tree-trunk table with a Picasso vase resting on it nonchalantly. The Navaho Room is linked to the Evelyn by a corridor dominated by a suspended and illuminated ceiling of blown glass shapes. The Evelyn, named after a yacht sign found in an antiques shop, is a long dining room. One of the boats originally built here is hung up

on the ceiling beside a row of Chihuly chandeliers which add grandeur to the otherwise basic room. The tabletop is an 88-foot (26-metre) plank of Douglas fir from a tree felled on Vancouver Island, and the floor is splattered with paint from the various spontaneous outbreaks of painting to which Chihuly is prone.

A door at the end of the dining room leads to the guest quarters. The walls of this split-level dining and bed area are decorated with punched-zinc squares and the bathroom with similar panels in copper. The bathroom has a Perspex sunken bath which has been plumbed in over an illuminated arrangement of coloured chunks of glass, which Chihuly admits is 'a little bit glitzy'.

These glass chunks look savage and uncultivated in comparison to the garden of sculptural pieces that are laid in a similar underwater fashion in the nearby lap pool. Beyond the pool a plain white door opens into a corridor and a short stroll brings you back to the studio, the furnaces, the magic wands of glass and the various jars of ores and resins that give this artist magician's glass its fabulous, distinctive colouring and patterns.

FOLLOWING PAGES, LEFT: The guest bathroom is decorated with punched-copper panels and a special Chihuly bath.

RIGHT: Sculptural glassworks are arranged above a glass panel in the ceiling of a passageway.

BELOW: The top of each of the lavender painted panels in the dining room acts as a frame for a collection of portraits bought at markets and fairs locally and abroad. The furniture is a mix of Victorian and Georgian pieces.

RIGHT: On the mantel of the dining room fireplace there is a display of old scientific sample jars containing examples of dried arable crops. On the right, a pair of double doors folds back to show the sitting room beyond.

northern territory

For many years Vicky Pepys and her husband Simon Young had high-speed lives in London. She worked as an account director at Lynne Franks Public Relations and he was design assistant to fashion designer Betty Jackson. Today they live in Northumberland in a colourful and characterful house that they have carefully renovated with their own interpretation of country style.

When Simon's career brought him to Northumbria, the couple sold their south London home and moved to the rural outskirts of Newcastle. Here they found an old, part-eighteenth-century, stone-built house with 8 acres (3 hectares) of fields. Over the years they have carefully restored and modernized the two-storey house, making each room an individual feature. With the help of family, friends and local craftsmen they removed the inappropriately modern metal double-glazed windows and replaced them with traditional wooden frames. An upper floor was added over a flat-roofed 1960s single-storey extension, and a weather-protective, Northumbrian-style porch was placed around the front door. The exterior is as true to the local style as possible, but inside the decoration is far from it. The back door opens into a boot-lined, green-and-cream porch and a stone-flagged lobby-cum-utility room. At the end is a walk-in pantry with each shelf neatly trimmed by cut-out paper borders. Outside the pantry a single stone step takes you up into the kitchen.

The kitchen is vibrant: the walls and some of the free-standing cupboards are painted a vivid shade of orange. Even the cool steel facade of the large semi-professional range recessed into the old fire hearth, now lined with steel cladding, does little to cool or detract from the bright colour. Next to the cooker is a commercial Coke refrigerator rescued from a Greek restaurant in Soho. Opposite, tucked in under the rise of the staircase to the upper floor, is a 1963 Wurlitzer Lyric jukebox. The radiators throughout the house were salvaged from a hospital in Burnley and the stone flags at this side of the house once covered the floors of a factory in Lancashire. Accessories come from junk shops in venues as widely spread as Chicago and Tooting Bec. At the windows orange-painted, wooden-panelled shutters are used instead of curtains. The couple felt that colour was important in the house because it is so often dark and rainy outside. From the kitchen a door leads to a narrow hall, with the staircase on the left and front door and porch on the right.

On the other side of the hall is the lavender-panelled dining room. Each of the upper panels is filled with a portrait, mostly bought from flea markets and local shops. The furniture in here, a Georgian dining table and Victorian dining chairs, have come from their families and the tall candlesticks were bought at an Indian shop in London.

Small double doors open from the lavender room to an expanse of almond-white sitting room, with three tall windows looking out over the fields beyond. The wall opposite the windows is painted in sky blue. This was the last room to be decorated and Vicky and Simon were desperate to

be clean after years of living with dust and rubble, so they opted for white. The floor is a reclaimed maple dance floor from Yorkshire and the mix-and-match sofas and chairs have been given uniform loose covers of white cotton. They returned to true colour-filled form for the small hallway just off the sitting room, which is panelled and painted a vivid bubble-gum pink. To one side is a pistachio-green cloakroom.

Upstairs, in the new addition built over the 1960s sitting-room extension, is a spacious high-ceilinged bedroom painted in buttercup yellow with three long windows overlooking the fields. The ceiling is studded with tiny halogen lights scattered, constellation-like, across the ceiling. En suite is a buff-coloured bathroom. Another bathroom is located at the other end of this corridor, and this time the walls and tiles are white but the central light and light over the handbasin have different, vivid-coloured glass shades. There are two more bedrooms on this upper floor, one in shades of dusky pink and mouse brown. The second room, painted in chartreuse green and yellow, is Vicky's office.

Vicky and Simon have traded in their hectic London lives, but the influences of their years in the fashion business can clearly be seen in their colourful home.

LEFT: In the kitchen a shelf of utensils and old enamel jugs hangs above a refurbished meat safe which supports more enamelware and antique weighing scales.

ABOVE: This sunny yellow bedroom was built on top of the single-storey 1960s extension. Pieces of period-style furniture give the room a comforting feel.

FAR LEFT: The long, high-ceilinged living room displays part of the collection of lighthouses which inspired the print of the materials used to upholster the armchairs on either side of the fireplace.

LEFT: Red-and-white commercial canvas awning has been glued to the walls and made into a shower curtain in the second bathroom. This room also has a nautical theme.

waterside getaway

Tony Baratta's weekend home is a picturesque Long Island fishing cottage, built in 1952. His intensely coloured and nostalgically decorated house is about an hour and a half's drive from the Manhattan offices of the interior design company Diamond Baratta, which he co-founded.

Tony Baratta's green-painted timber house is raised on stilts and set back, down a dirt-track road, from the shingle shoreline and silvery waters of Great Peconic Bay. It is close enough to New York to be easily accessible, but Tony wanted it to feel very far away from city life so he filled it with colour, starting by painting all the floors fire-engine red.

Although he bought the house fifteen years ago, Tony has done little internal structural alteration because he didn't want to interfere with the charm the building already had. Externally he developed the plot, adding a swimming pool and deck to the back and a porch to the front.

Wooden steps lead up from the stony path to the house and stop outside the enclosed porch. Immediately inside the doorway and its fly-screen panel there is a huge combined seat and coatstand where jackets can be hung and boots kicked off. Across the room is a long table and hickory stick-style chairs arranged beneath a large Stars and Stripes flag. Other furniture on this long veranda includes a couple of old, well-worn and mellow Adirondack chairs with their relaxing sloping backs and broad wooden arms.

Two separate sets of doors lead through the original outer wall of the house and into the living room, which has white walls and a high-pitched roof. There is a kitchen area at one end and in the middle of the room an upholstered seating arrangement centred around the fireplace. Opposite the fireplace is a built-in bookcase that almost glows from the shelves filled with hundreds of yellow-covered copies of National Geographic magazine. The end wall of the room is mostly taken up by a huge gun cabinet that Tony bought from an antiques shop in Massachusetts. Arranged on the remaining wall space are a framed selection of old black-and-white photographs of the National Parks of America.

The lighthouse collection, which is a dominant element of the room, was started inadvertently by the previous owners of the house, who gave Tony a model as a gift. The rest have been given by friends or bought by him. To the left at the back of the sitting room is the den.

The den is a wood-panelled room which is made even more forest-like by the deep-green roller blinds at the windows. The darkness is lifted by the upholstered cushions on the sofa and chairs, which are covered in a bright fish print. The only windowless wall is arranged with a collection of framed paint-by-numbers pictures, many carefully filled in by Tony's brother when they were children.

Next door to the den is a small bathroom with 1950s wallpaper portraying children playing all-American games such as baseball and box-karting. Beyond is the guest bedroom with an aviation-inspired scheme. From the ceiling, which is painted grey-and-white checkerboard, a large model aeroplane is suspended, and above the bedhead is a Flying Service emblem. An oversized rocking chair sits by a table in the window and across the bottom of the bed is a painting of a rowing boat.

On the far side of the spare bedroom is another bathroom decorated with red-and-white commercial awning canvas which has been glued to the walls and made into a matching shower curtain. The decorative theme in here is nautical, with a mirror in a wooden anchor frame and other items of sailing insignia.

The last room, Tony's bedroom, has a cowboy theme. The walls are clad with timber poles, giving the appearance of a log cabin. The head and footboard of the bed are padded in leather fixed with brass studs. Tony's initials appear in a studded oval, like a cowboy's brand, on the footboard. A bedside table is made from unfinished silver birch complete with papery bark, and a model of a cowboy with a lasso forms the lampbase.

A line of windows at the foot of the bed has roller blinds made from old maps, and the wall above is decorated with elaborate dress holsters and guns. The pillow and duvet covers are in a Diamond Baratta print of a log cabin in a pine forest with a river running by and a man in a canoe paddling past.

But Tony's home is not just a relaxing and fun place to be; it is also a source of inspiration. Sitting under the Stars and Stripes on the front porch, he doodles and muses on new fabric designs. 'The house also doubles as a sort of design laboratory. I try things out here,' he says. This casually but cleverly decorated home embraces elements of the great American past in its decor, making a welcoming and happy place in which to unwind; and being so relaxed it is also a place where creative thoughts may be nurtured.

LEFT: The long dining table is under an American flag in the porch, which was an addition added by Tony after he bought the house. Hickory chairs are arranged around the table, and an Adirondack chair sits in the foreground.

FOLLOWING PAGES, LEFT: The main bedroom has log-cabin-style panelling on the wall. The bedhead and footboard have been covered in leather and embellished with stud patterns to endorse the cowboy theme of the room.

RIGHT: The guest bedroom's aviation theme is clearly indicated by the large model aeroplane hanging from the grey-and-white checkered ceiling and the antique flying service badge above the bed.

converted

PREVIOUS PAGES: From the seating area of Dominic Richards's converted home, the view through the aperture is of the kitchen and dining room beyond.

FAR LEFT: The lap pool, in a glass-panelled extension, is joined to the side of the lower-level sitting room by tall window-like openings. The pool area is made to appear to be part of the room beyond.

LEFT: An open-tread staircase leads past a tall window decorated with a ceramic sculpture and an Oriental seat. The open design of the stairs allows light from both levels to illuminate the stairwell.

east meets west

Near the Bastille in Paris, there is a late-nineteenth-century building with a contemporary interior where East meets West. This is the home of the Japanese-born fashion designer Kenzo, whose distinctive style blends fashions of the Orient and the Occident, setting elegant pieces of period-style French furniture beside contemporary pieces of Chinese ceramics in architecturally elegant and understated rooms.

Like the clothes that Kenzo designs, his home is a mix of many cultures and inspirations. The house was designed and converted over ten years ago by French architect Xavier de Castella and Japanese designer Kenji Kawabata, and is a combination of contemporary glass-and-steel constructions with bamboo and paper screens and tatami matting. Kenzo wanted a home that was peaceful and comfortable and, because he didn't go to the country at weekends, he needed it to have the feeling of a holiday home. All the rooms have a different ambience so that when you walk through them it is as though you are travelling.

Entering into Kenzo's private world is an expedition in itself. From the street you pass through typical Parisian large painted wooden doors into a small courtyard and then through a glass-panelled opening into a larger inner yard. In front there is a wall of teakwood cladding and in the centre a tiny concealed entrance, so low that you stoop to pass through.

Once through the door, you walk along a raised pathway to the large pivoting panel that opens into the house. There are really three houses in one. Part of the house is designed with large rooms for entertaining and parties, another area is for more intimate, everyday living and the third is a perfect Japanese tea house. These are built on three staggered levels around a central courtyard well, filled with clumps of bamboo, which gives light and a green outlook to all the rooms with their glass-panelled walls.

To the right of the main entrance is a large living room dominated by three daybeds. This double-height room contains a vast array of sculptures, contemporary framed mirrors, paintings by Bastiat and Cocteau and a view over a small rear Zen courtyard with raked silver sand and pebbles.

The balcony to one side of this tall room contains Kenzo's simple bedroom with a low futon bed on tatami matting and a huge TV. Next to his bedroom is his book-lined study dominated by a large painting called *Divine*

Message by Ouathara, a friend of Bastiat, leather chairs by Christian Liaigre, who once had offices in the same building as Kenzo, and a huge desk covered with crayons and paints.

Beside the lower sitting room is a large kitchen with a dining area, and these rooms provide the formal entertaining section of the house. Above, leading from the study, is a smaller, more intimate kitchen and dining room with sliding-wood-and-white-paper screens that can be closed to create a division between the two spaces. Sliding opaque glass windows in the internal wall open to give views over the second, smaller sitting room and the indoor lap pool below.

On the other side of the lower sitting room, large glass panels look out over an Oriental garden and pond filled with Koi carp. The tree- and pebble-filled garden also extends in front of the Tea House, which is the third part of Kenzo's home and the most Japanese.

The main room of the Tea House is furnished with a low table and woven rattan seats. A small side room is where Kenzo likes to sleep in the summer and behind it, in the body of the main house, is a black marble Jacuzzi and a cherrywood-lined disrobing room. Throughout the many rooms of the house there are fresh flowers, candles and incense burners. The flowers are a reminder of Kenzo's childhood in Japan and the patterns on the kimonos worn by his mother and sisters.

Another theme running through the furnishings and artefacts is the elephant. A large wooden elephant statue in the entrance hall was discovered on a visit to Bangkok, and he subsequently bought the chairs by the pool and an Aubusson carpet with an elephant motif. Friends then started giving him presents with elephant embellishments or designs, and so the collection grew.

Kenzo's home, like his vast fashion empire, is constantly changing. Not only does he oversee the creation of seasonal collections for his men's, women's and children's accessories, but every three or four months he likes to alter his living spaces, moving furniture and accessories around to suit the seasons and outlook.

This spacious house has three distinct living areas, Japanese, public and private, as well as three separate styles of decoration – Oriental, contemporary and classic. However, the rooms link and flow coherently around the courtyards, wells and gardens which give this city house a very pastoral outlook. Many of the rooms are very simply decorated, and in these spaces the Oriental influence is at its strongest. In the more public spaces, contemporary art and furniture, blended with a few select pieces of antique European furniture and artefacts, make another distinct but harmonious statement.

LEFT: The Oriental garden and pond can be seen through the sliding screen doors of the Tea House, which is minimally furnished with tatami matting, low seats and a simple table.

FOLLOWING PAGES, LEFT: The back marble Jacuzzi bath is in a room at the back of the Tea House and has a long window overlooking one of the smaller bamboo-filled water gardens.

RIGHT: The warm, richly coloured cherrywood disrobing room is between the Tea House and the Jacuzzi. The modern, clean lines of this room are sympathetic to the Oriental simplicity of the other Tea House rooms.

RIGHT: Against the back wall of the kitchen is a home-made dresser with drawers constructed from old wine boxes and varying depths of shelving screwed onto brackets on the bare brick.

FAR RIGHT: The end wall of the third floor open-plan room, which contains living, dining, snooker and kitchen areas, is furnished with a grand piano and Hockney prints arranged around an unframed mirror.

The converted warehouse that Norman Ackroyd has made his home has had several previous uses, having been a hop store, a leatherworks and finally an Italian food warehouse. The old building is now not only his home, it is also his studio and printing works, and at times it is difficult to see where work ends and home begins in this unusual living and working space.

From street level you enter a small passage, which in turn leads to an open-plan printing room with the large metal press on which Norman's engravings are reproduced. Well-worn wooden stairs in the far corner of the room lead past a collection of miners' lamps, a memory of the mining industry around the city of Leeds where Norman was brought up.

At the top of the stairs is the official studio space with sheaves of paper hanging from the ceiling and a drawing board set up by the window at the front of the room. To the back of the room a daybed provides a place of rest and contemplation. Another narrow passageway and staircase lead to the next floor where the library and picture storage fit in among his children's bedroom and bathrooms.

More stairs rise up to the third floor, which is the main living space. This huge area is made to feel even larger because of the lofty pitched roof supported by hefty wooden beams. The warm red exposed-brick walls echo the utilitarian past of the building, and shafts of light criss-cross the room from the arched windows on either side.

At the end of the room nearest the stairs sits a Steinway grand piano. Norman says that for many years, rather than having the ambition of owning an expensive car, he had longed for a good piano. When one of his daughters took lessons and started to play, he decided that it was the right time to buy his piano, but as it couldn't be brought in by the narrow winding staircases it had to be lifted by crane through a window on this upper floor.

Also at this end of the room are prints by his art college contemporaries, who included David Hockney. Norman

an artist's eyrie

Norman Ackroyd is an artist and professor of print at the Royal Academy of Arts, and his work includes large public sculptures and moody, evocative landscape prints. His home and studio are in a converted warehouse near London Bridge where many of the original features have been kept and utilized in the construction of this unconventional residence.

remembers Hockney printing one of the posters on the table beside him. Alongside these noted artworks is an unframed mirror and a ladder that can be moved around to give access to various high-level shelves and bookcases.

In the centre of the room the original industrial winch sits by the double doors that once opened out over the street below. A pair of smaller doors that originally concealed a hoist to the floor beneath now opens to reveal a shallow cupboard which holds snooker balls and cues. The nearby snooker table has a dual use and is easily converted into a dining table when a large sheet of wood is placed on top.

The kitchen at the far end of the room is separated by a low wooden-panelled wall. Above it a suspended shelf is crammed with ingredients and cooking utensils. Behind this area of worktop is a dresser made from a base found at a local second-hand shop and shelves screwed onto brackets on the wall. Norman had a sheet of slate cut to fit the top of the base unit and built the wooden drawers himself from old wine boxes with screw-in handles.

Passing the snooker/dining table, wooden stairs lead to the fourth floor, which is an eyrie-like later addition on the corner of the building and contains his bedroom, bathroom and rooftop terrace garden. Under the apex of the roof, on a wall covered with sheets of white paper, are more works in progress, and to the right is a small drawing of a man's head by Castiglione. Norman describes this as his inspiration, a picture that he studies from time to time and one that gives him much pleasure.

Norman admits that when the urge to paint comes over him he works until the small hours of the morning, and when he does finally sleep he covers his eyes with a set of airline eyeshades because the large skylight windows above his bed remain curtainless. The light from these window is invaluable when he works, and that takes priority over his domestic needs in this converted workspace.

Norman Ackroyd's home is a very individual space. It is colourful, not in the sense that many shades of paint have been used but in the sense that it is lively, interesting and full of character. It has evolved around one man's needs and has accommodated his artistic lifestyle with space to spare.

LEFT: Norman's fourth-floor bedroom and sometimes daylight studio is illuminated through a glass-panelled roof. Because he doesn't restrict the light with blinds or curtains, he often has to sleep wearing eyeshades.

self-improvement

Mark Budden, director of a product-and-design-development company, is passionate about buildings and construction. This passion lured him into spending two and a half years transforming part of an ink factory in the east of London into a two-level, industrially inspired, ultra-modern family home.

RIGHT: The mezzanine level, suspended above the lower living space, contains the bathroom and two bedrooms. The main bedroom shown here can be concealed behind walls of heavy cotton curtain panels.

FOLLOWING PAGES, LEFT: The open-plan living space contains the kitchen, dining and seating areas. In keeping with the previous industrial use of the building, pipes and structural elements have been left exposed.

RIGHT: The curved glass-brick wall of the mezzanine-level bathroom is up-lit at night by a row of spotlights in the floor. Speakers have also been wired into this room so that relaxing music can be played at bathtime.

Mark Budden was so taken with the structure of the inkworks, designed in 1931 by Captain Stanley Peach (the architect of the Centre Court at Wimbledon), that he did as much as he could to retain the character of the original building. Among the distinctive features are the tall north-facing windows, originally designed to allow daylight, untainted by sun, to flood into the large rooms so that the ink-makers could match colours accurately. The brick walls have been left bare but cleaned so that their rich colouring adds to the warmth of the rooms; controls for the heating system have been left exposed and pristine, polished piping is proudly on show, all endorsing the industrial heritage.

When, in 1992, the building was sold and subdivided into units, Mark bought a 1,200-square-foot (110-square-metre) shell. He sectioned off the tall space by installing a mezzanine level, constructed from large metal beams and partially suspended from the roof joists, on which he camped while he got on with the job of converting the space around him.

The living and eating areas are located on the lower level. On one side of the entrance corridor, with its natural sisal floor covering, he has constructed a row of deep cupboards which contain a lavatory and cloakroom, a coat-hanging space and a laundry room. The latter houses the washer and drier, horizontal rows of drying lines and a fold-down ironing board which clips up against the wall when not in use.

Opposite the door that conceals the laundry is the main living room, subdivided into the kitchen, dining and sitting areas. The kitchen is L-shaped, practical and understated and mainly steel with a glass splashback. The floor in this area is covered with individually selected sandstone tiles. At the end of the kitchen is the dining area and beside that the seating area, with a large comfortable sofa and armchairs.

The windows that run along behind this and the dining area are the tall north-facing ones once used by the ink-makers. Mark tracked down the manufacturers of the original winder mechanisms that opened the high windows and had the whole winding system overhauled. The floor in this living area is beech, chosen for its knotty character, which Mark felt would also complement the rough texture of the surrounding brick walls.

But the apartment is not all hard edges and industrial finishes. The mezzanine floor, now reached by a metal-and-wood staircase, leads to a storage and study area concealed behind flush wooden doors where files and references for the work done on the apartment are stored. Next to it is a bedroom, now Mark's son's room, which can be made more private by drawing a colourful curtain that leaves a corridor space outside. In the corner of this upper level is the bathroom, made with a curved wall of glass bricks. Speakers are wired into the bathroom wall so that music can be played during a relaxing bath, and uplighters sunken into the floor cast shafts of light up the walls which, at nighttime, make the bathroom seem like a space pod.

Further round on the mezzanine, over the kitchen and dining area, is the main bedroom. As with Mark's son's room, where you might expect solid walls there are curtains, but these can be pulled back to enhance the feeling of light and space. The bedhead is built with concealed light switches and storage units that slide neatly into the casing of the bedhead. All the cupboards and units have been left with space above and below so that they appear to float.

Towards the end of his work on the conversion, Mark married Krystina. When she moved in she insisted on more storage and cupboard space for her clothes, so Mark added finely finished MDF (medium-density fiberboard) cupboards and a tall, mirror-fronted cabinet in the bathroom. Later still, with the arrival of their son Charlie, even more storage space was needed, so again Mark went back to his drawing board.

Mark's home is a true labour of love. It took him two and a half years to transform it from an empty shell—first to a bachelor pad and finally into a customized family home. The apartment is a thoroughly contemporary space and, despite the amount of hard metal and brick surfaces on show, is neither cold nor inhospitable.

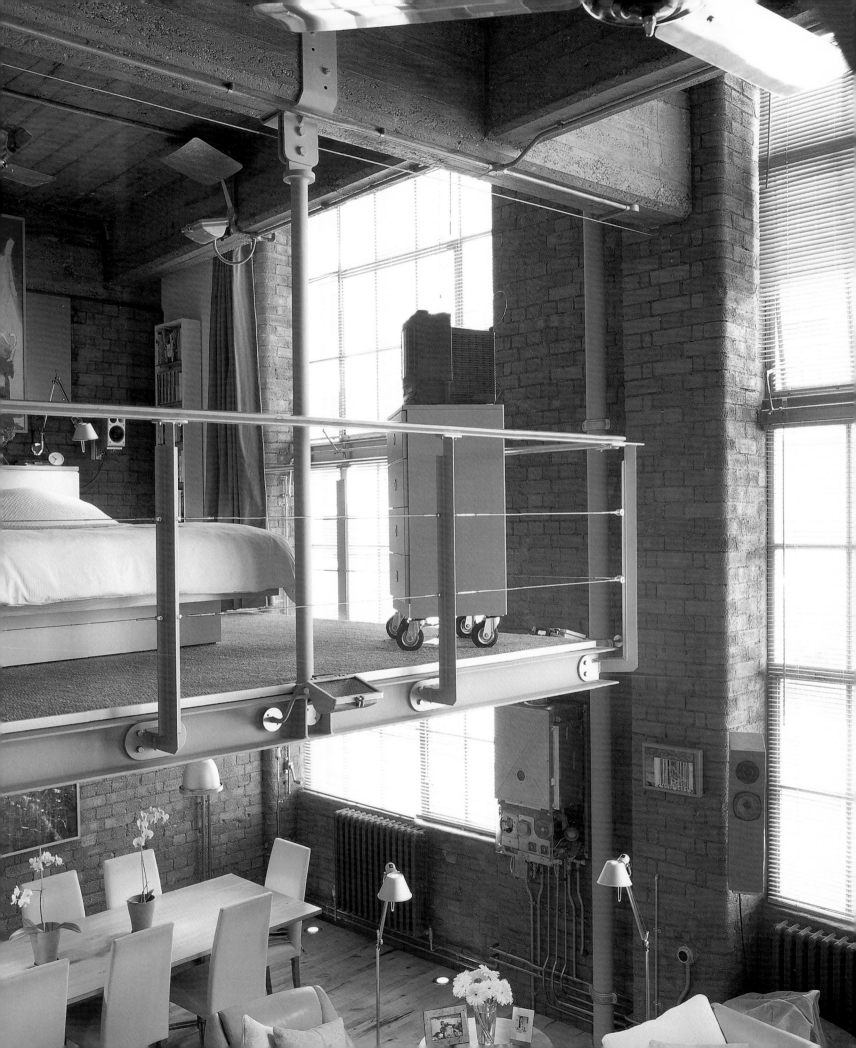

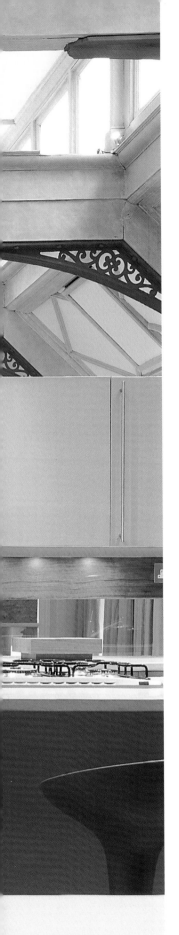

urban retreat

Architectural designer and businessman Dominic Richards's east London home is a recycled Victorian workspace. The large room that now houses his coolly tailored, twenty-first-century living area was once a steam-filled, bustling hive of activity, with industrial chimneys and flues exiting through the high-pitched roof. The generous proportions of this room now easily accommodate his ample-sized pieces of contemporary furniture.

Dominic Richards wasn't looking for a home when he happened to pass by a disused building in London's East End. But being curious he went through the door and said then and there that he would buy it, and a few weeks later he moved in. Having studied at the Prince of Wales's architectural school, he has a trained eye for evaluating space and could instantly see the potential that the back section of the old building offered. Some work had already been undertaken by a developer who had subdivided the upper level into a series of small box-like rooms to contain the kitchen and bathroom, with a bedroom 'box' where the kitchen is now and a smaller sitting area on the other side. The beams had been painted black and gold in a mock Tudor style and the floor was covered in imitation wood. All this was speedily removed.

Dominic's home is an urban retreat, a quiet space at the back of the Victorian building, away from the traffic and noise of the busy main road in front. To decorate it he used an 'Earth Minimalism' scheme, which he describes as being not harsh or artificial but contemporary, with traditional materials.

From a small lobby a door opens into a large living space with a high ceiling. Immediately in front of the door is the sitting area with generous-sized sofas so that lots of people can sit there. They are covered in a soft, knobbly fabric reminiscent of natural lambswool, and the polished oak floor is enhanced by a cream tufted rug. The tall windows along the far wall, with their original ceramic cream-glazed brick arches, are softened with natural linen curtains.

To the left of the front door a pair of featureless, plain-coloured doors conceal a large, deep storage cupboard, beside which a round tower-like column contains a shower room, lavatory and an unusual sloping stone sink. As well as being a useful space, this column also has a decorative impact. The internal curve of the wall has recessed spotlights in the floor

LEFT: This overall view of the upper level shows the dining table in the foreground, the kitchen in the centre and the sitting section beyond. The high ceiling with original wrought-iron beams adds to the grandeur of the room.

LEFT: The far side of the kitchen's island unit doubles as a breakfast bar. For more formal entertaining there is the refectory-style table made from oak and limestone.

RIGHT: To the left of the sofa are the doors concealing a deep storage cupboard, and to the right the column-like exterior of the pod that contains the shower, lavatory and basin. The pod also becomes a lighting feature at night.

and at night a pool of light shines up through the glass roof of the shower and onto the ceiling above.

The sitting area is separated from the kitchen and dining section by a free-standing wall that has a narrow central opening just above the worktop. The kitchen is streamlined and well thought out so that Dominic, a keen cook who loves to entertain, can talk to guests in the sitting room or around the dining table as he cooks. The kitchen units are all faced with sealed MDF (medium-density fiberboard), the worktops are of limestone and the facings above are made of Indian laurel, in keeping with the simple, almost monastic look that Dominic aspired to. On the walls at either end of this tranquil, understated space are two groups of four large-format photoprints by Max Malandrino of Super Neo Design Concepts. The imposing colourful graphic images are in contrast to the calm setting and bring a glimpse of the contemporary world inside the Victorian walls of this once utilitarian space.

Beside the kitchen, running parallel to the island section of work surface, is the dining area. A specially commissioned refectory-style dining table has been made from part of an oak tree blown down during the storms of 1987. The date rings were counted and it was estimated that the tree had been planted around 1650. A section of the ancient wood has been set into the centre of two broad strips of limestone. In contrast, the high-tech wireless system enables a laptop computer to be used anywhere in the apartment without having to plug it into a phone socket. There is also an integrated stereo system so that the TV sound, CD and radio work in each area on the two levels.

Beyond the table and dining area, broad stairs lead down to the lower-level bedroom and bathroom. This floor, in the old basement store of the works, is mainly below ground level, so the walls have been left plain and the furnishings simple to maximize the feeling of space and light.

The building that now houses Dominic's home has been transformed from an industrial workspace into a tranquil, modern domestic apartment while respecting its heritage and the original structure and features.

future predictions

Dutch-born Li Edelkoort is one of the world's leading style predictors, revealing the trends of the future to fashion retailers, car manufacturers and flower companies. Her home, a three-storey house on the edge of the Périphérique, Paris's major ring road, has been converted from a prosaic workshop and dwelling into a refined and gracious living space.

LEFT: In front of the kitchen sink is an old chopping block, which is used as a work surface.

Although Li Edelkoort travels extensively lecturing and researching for her business, when she returns home her roots are firmly fixed in the house that has been her base for the last eight years. With her clever ideas about what the next trend will be and her strong links to those who create them, you might be forgiven for thinking that her home would be a shrine to futuristic style, but in fact it reflects much more her love of art and crafts.

Behind the high, unprepossessing exterior walls that form the corner of the street outside lies a small, flower-filled, cobbled courtyard. Around this courtyard, in an L shape, are two buildings each with their own front door. In the short leg of the L, in what used to be a workshop, a door leads to Li's bedroom and bathroom, while in the other building the door opens beside her study, once another workroom, and a staircase leads up to the main living space above.

On the upper levels the two houses are linked externally by a terrace and walkway, which means that to go from one part of her home to the other Li always has to go outside. She doesn't seem to mind this strange arrangement, saying that the experience is like a journey.

The living area of the first floor of the larger building has one wall of floor-to-ceiling windows which overlook the courtyard below. These windows give the room a feeling of space and a modern appearance. The walls here are white and the floor is painted black, as they are in most of the other rooms in the houses.

The furnishings are simple and include a couple of grey-flannel-covered chairs on a grey-and-yellow, hand-stitched felt rug placed at one end of the room, and a deep chocolate-brown, velvet-covered sofa and a hide-covered chair at the other. Artefacts collected on her travels are scattered rather than arranged, and vary from a contemporary Italian painting and an old Venetian mirror to a carved wooden chain by a Korean artist and a hand-thrown pot from Africa.

An archway at the end of the sitting room, almost in the right angle of the L, opens into the spacious kitchen and dining space. At the far end of the room, under a large skylight, is a steel-clad sink unit on tall metal legs with open shelving underneath. In front of the sink is an old wooden chopping block, which acts as an extra section of work surface, with more shelves of pottery, china and glass on either side. A steel-covered fridge dominates the empty wall between the food preparation and eating areas, creating a nominal divide.

In the dining area a long, narrow table is surrounded by carved ethnic stools. These stools, in various sizes, can be

LEFT: Artefacts collected by Li on her travels include this giant carved wooden chain.

RIGHT: Li's courtyard bedroom is understated and comfortable, with a fireplace and deep recesses for relaxing in.

found all around the house and are used for a variety of tasks from supporting the TV to acting as a bedside table. The dining table is set with an African indigo-printed cloth and unusual plain white Moroccan pottery.

From the far side of the living room another staircase leads up to the top floor and a spare bedroom and bathroom. Also at this level is the external metal walkway which runs across the two buildings. At the far side, over towards the living room, there is a tiled terrace where another long table provides the perfect setting for al fresco dining with friends in warm weather.

The neutral white background decoration is continued in the furnishing of Li's courtyard bedroom, and is warmed slightly by the inclusion of cream-coloured throws, cushions and fabrics. A fire surround has been built along one wall and

incorporates two deep recesses which are filled with thick-knit cushions for lounging.

The bed is layered with simple printed cotton sheets and light wool throws, while the mats on the concrete screed floor are hand-woven cotton appliquéd with rows of metal sequins which jingle slightly when walked on. The en-suite bathroom is also a simply decorated room with white-painted and tiled walls and a practical concrete screed floor.

Li Edelkoort's home is a relaxing place to be in. She predicts that the twenty-first century will be a time when contrasting styles fuse. Decorative will mix with minimalism, old things with new and people will strive to find inner space and calm. Examples of all of these predictions can already be seen at work in her own home, so perhaps this really is the look of the future.

LEFT: The hand-painted, blue-panelled dressing room opens off the main bedroom on the second floor in the original part of the house. The soft colours and decorative panelwork on the doors give the room a traditional appearance.

RIGHT: The long windowless corridor in the newly converted upper storey of the house is where the old and new parts of the house meet. The doors on the right conceal a kitchen and walk-in wardrobes.

The mix of traditional and contemporary style displayed in Anna Zegna's home is also part of her working life. The Ermenegildo Zegna company is traditional (at the mills, lengths of fabric are individually cut with scissors to fulfil each order), but the company is best known for its sharp contemporary men's fashions. At home, traditional and contemporary have come together more gradually. When Anna and her husband Franco Ferraris bought their house more than a decade ago, it was initially adapted and decorated to be a conventional family home for themselves and their children. Most of the building dates from the beginning of the eighteenth century, and many of the old floors and doors have been restored. Anna's first cousin, architect Andrea Zegna, enclosed middle sections of the open terraces of the ground and middle floors to create corridors, so that each bedroom now has its own entrance rather than being interconnected, and there is also an enclosed passage between the kitchen and dining room.

On the lower level the work included transforming the original store and stables into a kitchen and dining room. A large reception hall separates this working part of the house from the formal sitting room and library beyond. The sitting room and library are richly decorated in traditional style with cushions, side tables draped with woollen throws, Victorian armchairs, sofas and antique china ornaments.

Stone stairs lead up from the reception hall to the middle floor and the bedrooms and bathrooms, which again have a firmly traditional style of decor. The couple's son's room is blue and white with a long cupboard fitted with hand-painted Venetian panels. Their daughter's is a homage to the Bloomsbury group of British writers and painters and is decorated with borders and patterns inspired by Charleston. At the end of the corridor overlooking the remaining open section of terrace is the master bedroom, study, dressing room and bathroom. A single door leads into the dressing room, which is lined with hand-painted blue cupboards. To the left is the apple-green bathroom and on

ancient and modern

Anna Zegna is the communications director and one of the third generation of her family to work in the textile business founded by her grandfather, Ermenegildo Zegna. Her home in the Piedmont region of northern Italy is an intriguing mix of styles, part beautifully restored traditional home and part modern, minimalist apartment.

RIGHT: The comfortable period-style sitting room with the library and study beyond are in the early-eighteenth-century part of the house. The painted beam ceiling is one of the remaining original features.

FAR LEFT: The den with its unusual pivoting door is the last room at the end of the long, modern roof conversion on the top floor of the family home. The sofa is upholstered in a woollen men's suiting fabric, endorsing the masculine theme of the room.

LEFT: A modern wall-hung handbasin is suspended from a column that is set forward, away from the sloping ceiling of the roof in the bathroom on the recently converted top floor.

the far side the simply furnished bedroom with Franco's study in a recess at one side. The windows on this side of the house look out on an uninterrupted view of the village of Savaro nestling in a valley.

Another flight of stairs leads up to the top floor. A dark brown panelled door, similar to all the others, opens into a long windowless corridor which is the entrance to the new part of the house designed by architect Luisa Bocchietto. This upper level, formerly an unused attic space, was converted recently because Anna felt that she wanted a cleaner, quieter place, a change of pace from the rest of the family home on the floors beneath. In the corridor what appears to be a maple-panelled wall is in fact a series of cupboards with touch-release catches. The first cupboard houses a kitchen, the others are walk-in wardrobes with fixed rails on either side.

During the day the plain white-painted walls of the roof-top rooms reflect the light from the skylight windows

overhead and a number of small side windows. At night recessed wall lights and light fittings under shelves provide a relaxing diffuse illumination.

At the end of the main corridor is a bathroom with sauna, shower and modern handbasin. Outside, the corridor turns sharply to reveal another long passage. In the first section is a large cream contemporary sofa by Antonio Citterio, a couple of throws from Zegna's home collection and two local handmade pots. Behind the sliding panels in the walls are a large-screen TV and the music system. In the next section is Anna's office with a leather-covered table and chair by Romeo Sozze. There are also step and bicycle machines against the wall and a computer on a metal storage system.

The final section is a small den with a pivoting door. This is Franco's space. A humidor keeps his cigars in perfect condition and a small sofa, covered in Ermenegildo flannel suiting, provides a place to sit and enjoy them.

FAR LEFT: The sitting room in the centre of the old church is set on a raised floor to bring the seating closer to the windows and daylight. The furniture includes an traditional Caithness chair on the left and an Orkney seat on the right.

LEFT: The dining area features a reconstructed communion table. The panelling on the lower half of the walls was made from wood reclaimed from other parts of the church.

highland retreat

A converted Georgian church in Midlothian, in south east Scotland, is home to harpist and glass engraver Alison Kinnaird and her husband Robin Morton, a musician who now runs a recording studio in the heart of the original Gothic-style church.

ABOVE: This bedroom is in what was the balcony of the Dundas gallery. The high, pointed Gothic windows, with detailed stone carving and leaded windows, are found throughout the building.

RIGHT: The main bedroom has a dramatic half-tester style bedhead constructed from the church's original finely decorated wooden pulpit. A chair with carved barley sugar twist frame is upholstered with hand-sewn tapestry.

The old church at Temple was once filled with a Presbyterian congregation of the families and staff of the nearby Dundas and Rosebery estates, but now the pews and balconies have been re-used to create a family home and workspace. Most of the interior fittings were recycled to form panelling and furniture, and much of the transformation was done by a Canadian woodworker friend who came over and spent a winter doing the conversion. The body of the church now contains the recording studio, where Robin works, and the sitting room. In the wings, bedrooms and a music room have been built into the space occupied by the former balconies of the Dundas and Rosebery staff.

Entering the house through the vine-filled porch, a recent addition, the first room you come to is the kitchen. This is a dark but cosy room with cupboards made out of the old pew doors. The gilt-painted numbers of the pews are still in evidence, but inside the cupboards, because the carpenter who constructed the kitchen couldn't bear to have the numbers on the outside as they were out of sequence. The

walls of this room are half panelled with more reclaimed wood and the table has been constructed from the original communion table. It was cut in half and the two sides joined together to form a shorter, wider surface.

Beyond the kitchen is the recording studio with its well-insulated walls and sound baffles. On the far side of the studio two steps lead up and into the sitting room where the floor has been raised to give a better view out of the windows. These large Gothic-style openings let in plenty of daylight and are in their original cast-iron frames, which are preferable to wood or lead which can warp and bend.

In the high-ceilinged sitting room a wood-burning stove radiates heat, and against the wall opposite an old organ rests between two cabinets filled with glass. One contains pieces of Alison's engraving, using glass blown locally in Galashiels. In the other there is a mixed collection of antique pieces picked up by Robin at auctions and sales. Among the many chairs in this room are fine examples of Scottish vernacular style. On the balcony above, the paraphernalia of the Temple records office overflows from a small adjacent room.

Stairs from the sitting room rise up to the Rosebery Gallery, now the music room. Another organ sits at the back and a collection of unusual instruments, including a long-handled fiddle, are on the wall and floor around it. The room also houses a selection of Alison's harps and Robin's accordions.

The door from the far end of the music room leads to a narrow corridor and the main bedroom. This large, light room has an internal window looking out over the sitting-room balcony and an external window with a view of the garden and the ruins of a twelfth-century church founded by the Knights Templar. The bed is under the inverted original elaborately carved wood pulpit. At the foot of the bed there is a wall of wardrobes with panelling featuring the Gothic arch that is such a commanding feature of all the external windows.

Further along the corridor, back towards the kitchen end of the church, are the bedrooms of the Mortons' grown-up children. Their daughter's room is in part of the Dundas gallery, and her dolls' house, built in the style of Kinkell Castle, still sits at the foot of the bed. On the landing outside their daughter's bedroom, by the top of the stairs leading down to the porch and kitchen, Alison has her studio, chosen for the quality of the light through yet another of the grand Gothic windows.

The unusual home that Alison and Robin have created provides them with space in which to live and work, pursuing their various careers in art and music. Between the old ecclesiastical stone walls is well-balanced harmony in the homely and comfortable ambience of the old church.

LEFT: The main doors to the house have porthole windows and an angular sail awning which acts as a protective porch. These doors open into the hallway, which was added when the external staircase was converted into an internal one.

RIGHT: John crow's-nest office in the apex of the roof. The ceiling and walls have been clad in tongue-and-groove boards, reminiscent of the clinker-built structure of boats.

shoreline shelter

Designer and builder John Rolf was born and brought up on the Isle of Wight. After a period in 'exile', living and working in London, he returned to the island where he bought and converted The Boat House. Making the most of the waterside location, he used large windows to maximize the beautiful views and recycled much of the original timber to construct a new house in an old shell.

When John Rolf bought the building that is now his home the ground, or more accurately water, level was still employed to store boats. The upper level had been used by a family as an occasional stop-over on summer nights, but to make it a full-time, habitable home John had to start from scratch. Not long after he moved in there was a force-ten gale and the whole building started to rock. To stabilize the structure, the frame of The Boat House had to be jacked up and a level foundation installed, covering the original slipway that came in from the shoreline.

The original end wall of the building finished halfway through what is now the living room, so John introduced two old wooden masts as pillar supports and extended the room, completing it with a wall of French windows. These windows look across to a small jetty on the far side of the estuary, and light on the water creates dappled patterns on the ceiling. The space had been open through to the roof with galleries on either side, each gallery bearing the name of the yacht or boat that had been stored there. The original beams were so substantial that rather than move them, John planned the walls and rooms to work around them and left most of the old brackets exposed.

Located in an area of special scientific interest where the shoreline and bird life is exceptional, the outside of the house has had a major influence on the decor inside. The history of the building, home to a sailmaking, yacht and boatbuilding business founded in 1816, also had an effect.

At the front, double doors with portholes are protected from the elements by a sail-like canvas covering. Inside, a large square hallway forms part of a new extension, and where an external staircase once stood a modern, internal one has been built. The floor in this area is covered with practical terra-cotta tiles, and a wall of cupboards, made from limed wood with weather-worn wooden handles, provides ample hanging space for boots and sou'westers. The glass-panelled wall opposite the doors admits natural light to illuminate the staircase and frames the view of the waterscape and boats beyond.

LEFT: Shells and flotsam and jetsam collected on shoreline walks add to the decoration of the bathroom en suite to the main bedroom. The clean white scheme enhances the feeling of the seaside location.

FAR LEFT: The newly extended rear section of the living room has a wall of sliding glass panels which lead out on to a small terrace reaching out over the water's edge.

To the right of the hall another pair of double doors with portholes leads into the main living space. This is a vast room, which John's partner Joan admits was a difficult space to furnish. At first the sofas were arranged in a linear fashion but it looked too formal, so they divided the space into smaller, more intimate sections with armchairs and a large sofa facing each other in front of the French windows. At the far side of the room a five-foot (one-and-a-half-metre) round window overlooks the rock garden and mill ponds beyond, its size and shape echoed by the round tables beneath it. Limed cupboards, recycled from a kitchen but now with the appearance of wood salvaged from the beach, provide storage space.

Behind the living area is the kitchen. Original timbers, treated to make them flame-retardant, are used as panelling. Off the kitchen is a small pantry, and in the area between the kitchen and living space an L-shaped configuration of old church pews, from a chapel in Cowes, is arranged around a small table. The back of the pew facing towards the hallway doubles as a bookcase. Beyond is a shower and cloakroom.

From the hallway, open-tread stairs lead to the first floor landing. To the front, French doors open out on to a sundeck which extends in front of the master bedroom. This room is light, white and minimally furnished with a walk-in wardrobe to one side and an en-suite bathroom. There is also a guest bedroom and bathroom. Another smaller flight of stairs leads to the top floor and John's crow's-nest office. A pair of cabin-style bunk beds for guests has been built against one wall.

Some people might have opted to build a new house by the water, but John has made his home a part of the shoreline. In the process, he has embraced the seaside spirit.

LEFT: A corner of Ungaro's study shows the vaulted stone ceiling and the stone fire surround. Rich tapestry hangings and upholstery warm the cool room and allude to Renaissance period style.

RIGHT: This small sitting room on the lower level is used for informal entertaining in the winter, and during the summer large doors open from here onto the terrace with its line of stone statues.

a dream home

When couture designer Emanuel Ungaro first visited his house in the south of France, he knew he would live there because he had seen it in a dream. But it took eleven years to transform the derelict twelfth-century chapel and hostel into a richly colourful and ornately decorated villa with allusions to Renaissance and Baroque styles.

When Emanuel Ungaro started looking for a place he could come to for an occasional break from the demands and pressures of his work in Paris, he came back to his roots. He was born and brought up in the nearby town of Aix-en-Provence where his father, an Italian by birth, was a tailor. When he finally came across this location with the derelict ancient buildings set amongst a few gnarled olive trees, he knew he had found the place. He was sure that it was his destiny to live here, because he had seen it in a dream and recognized it immediately.

After many years of painstaking work the Ungaros' home is now fully restored and transformed. The long, linear house has two storeys at the front, overlooking a Tuscan-style courtyard, and three at the back. The rooms at the front are used in the spring and autumn because they get most of the sun and are warm and pleasant. In the summer, when the heat becomes more intense, the family retreats to the other, cooler side of the building.

A few steps down from the chapel, overlooking the Tuscan courtyard, is a small shaded porch where they take breakfast on warm spring mornings. A door leads into a rich flame-red ante-room with a large open fireplace. To the left is Ungaro's book-filled study with bookcases built in under the restored but original vaulted ceilings. In the passageway beside the study, stone stairs lead up to the main bedroom, and opposite is a small family dining room, again with a vaulted ceiling. The floor here is of old brick laid in a herringbone pattern, and the decorative tablecloth is of appliquéd Indian fabric, a particular favourite of Ungaro's found elsewhere in the house used as bed quilts, covers and throws. Behind this room is a colourfully tiled 'winter' kitchen and to the side a door leads to a first floor terrace .

On the far side of the red ante-room and family dining room there is a long corridor, with a decorative plaster ceiling, leading to the principal salon. This room, with painted beams and a huge stone fireplace, is used for more formal entertaining. A carved marble staircase at one end curves up

LEFT: The grand principal salon has a cool marble floor and finely painted decorative wooden beams. The furniture is aligned to the centre of the substantial stone fireplace on the end wall.

FOLLOWING PAGES, LEFT: This view of the principal salon looks from the fireplace back towards the stairs that lead up to the second floor. The side walls of this room are dressed with richly decorated cabinets, console tables and gilded chairs.

RIGHT: The formal dining room is adjacent to the principal salon. The beams here are not so ornate, and the fireplace has finer pillars, yet it retains the rich colouring and style of the main room.

to the second floor where there are five bedrooms and bathrooms for visiting family and friends.

To the side of the decorative plaster hallway another staircase leads down to the lower floor where, on the right, there is another kitchen and scullery and on the left a small sitting room. Tall double doors lead from the sitting room to a large terrace. At one end of the terrace's lower level Ungaro has installed an old *lavoir* or washing tank. The cool, tinkling sound of the water in the shady enclave is seductive on a hot day. This second terrace with its row of stone statues, mature leafy trees and view over the countryside is where the family eats in the shade during the intense heat of the southern French summer.

Much of the interior of the house is furnished with Italian artefacts, such as intricately patterned and coloured scagliola tables, painted bow-fronted cabinets and rich, dark wood furniture, supplemented with things found at Parisian flea markets. Laura, Ungaro's wife, softens the rich, sometimes masculine style of the rooms with bunches of freshly picked herbs, often sage and rosemary, or bunches of vividly coloured roses bought at the local market, whose scent adds to the ambience.

Before he bought the house Ungaro had amassed a collection of doors, some carved, others panelled and a few painted. When the interior of the building was designed it was done so that the doors could be incorporated as built-in cupboards, doors between rooms and as faux panels. Essentially, the rooms were made to fit the doors rather than the doors to fit the rooms.

Ungaro is very much a hands-on man, overseeing the design and building, finding the artefacts and painstakingly assembling all the elements that have come together to create the grand, elegant and unique house that is his very private retreat from life in Paris.

LEFT: The view from the end sitting room to the kitchen is uninterrupted and naturally illuminated by daylight, which shines through the long section of glass wall and is a feature of the new design.

RIGHT: The landing on the first floor is as minimal and uncluttered as the rest of the house. The graphic lines of the architectural features make them appear almost sculptural.

uninterrupted space

Gareth and Miranda Thompson's oasthouse home in Kent dates from the 1880s, but the interiors are incontrovertibly modern. Small individual rooms were abandoned in favour of wide-open spaces, the rear wall was removed and replaced with glass, and the materials used to achieve this up-to-date style included concrete, sand-finished render and polycarbonate.

ABOVE: The main bathroom is minimally furnished with a bath, without traditional panelled sides, and a single white ceramic basin.

RIGHT: This detail shows one of the galvanized steel supports for the ducts which conceal old beams, pipes and wiring, and a section of the polycarbonate panels that have been used to create partition walls.

From the outside Gareth and Miranda Thompson's oast-house looks like many others you pass in the Kent countryside, apart from the missing conical oast tower which burnt down many years ago. But once through the small side door, it is clear that the Thompsons have a very different approach to living in a rural, barn-style building.

To achieve a barn conversion with a difference they worked with the architectural team Caruso St John, whose work they admired. Gareth knew that he wanted to avoid the standard barn conversion, which invariably divides the space into lots of little rooms, and he also wanted to break away from the general mould of predictable interiors. Initially they debated the option of using the height of the building to create a mezzanine floor but, on investigation, it was found that an inherent structural weakness made that impossible. Instead the architects designed a scheme that accentuated the length of the ground floor of the building. The front of the building remains exactly as it was, brick-built and with the

windows in the same positions. But along the back Adam Caruso and Peter St John took away the solid wall and replaced it with a large expanse of glass panels inset between solid timber uprights. This glass section brings light into the whole of the ground floor and gives a magnificent view of the garden and orchards beyond.

The internal open-plan scheme means that you stand in the kitchen at one end of the house and look through, past the cloakroom, entertainment room and dining area, to the sitting room at the other end, a wonderful feeling of uninterrupted space. Even the divisions that have been built do not restrict this line of vision because they partially, rather than wholly, intercept the main corridor space and are constructed from apparently lightweight component parts. The architects used a variety of materials on the interior, including those more often seen on the outside of a building.

Unattractive beams and supports, utilitarian pipes, cables and wires are all concealed in galvanized steel ducts of the sort found in industrial warehouses and factories. The hall, a square room around the large central sliding door at the front of the house, and the cloakroom have been created from polycarbonate panels, more often found on garden greenhouse roofs. This opaque material looks off-white and unusual in daylight, but at night concealed lights behind the panels shine through, providing a soft, diffuse light, illuminating the walls and making them appear almost immaterial.

The floor at this level is concrete, which is not as cold as it might seem because of the underfloor heating. The walls are rendered with a sand-textured finish which has a mellow, pleasant hue, while the ceiling is completely covered with natural wooden boards of a pale golden colour, giving an earthy, warm feel to the large space. All the floors upstairs are covered in the same wooden boards as the ground-floor ceilings, and all the walls are painted white. The ceilings in each of the top-floor rooms have retained some of the old timbers, renovated and painted. These beams are the only internal concession to the building's original construction.

Over the kitchen is the master bedroom which leads through to a bathroom and walk-in wardrobe. In the centre of the house, over the dining area, is their daughter's bedroom, and next to that is a study and finally a spare bedroom. The couple could have had more smaller rooms but they were wedded to the feeling of space so opted for fewer, larger rooms throughout.

When Gareth and Miranda moved into their new home, they sold most of their furniture and started afresh with pieces to suit its streamlined shape, following the dictum that 'less is more' and that less furniture leaves more space.

Suppliers

Joseph Ettedgui

(also Jules Haimovitz)

Furniture by Christian Liaigre

Tel: 00 331 53 63 3366

Deirdre Dyson

Carpet design and design service

331 Kings Road

London SW3 5ES

Tel: 020 7795 0122

www.deirdredyson.com

Ann Mollo

Garden Design

Tel: 020 7603 3762

email artifix@aol.com

Henry Dent-Brocklehurst

Designer Nick Esch

Tel: 020 8248 8162 or 0973 968 858

Architects Loates Taylor Shannon

11–12 Great Sutton Street

London SE1 4PU

Tel: 020 7357 7000

Cath Kidston

Shops:

8 Clarendon Cross

London W11 4AP

Tel: 020 7221 000

8 Elystan Street

London SW3 3NS

020 7584 3232

www.cathkidston.co.uk

Graham Fraser and Richard Nott

Stoneacre is a National Trust property in Otham, Kent.
The main house and gardens are open on Wednesdays
and Saturdays only from 2-6pm, April to October, or at
other times by appointment.
For information, tel: 01622 862871

Bradley Gardner

Details of properties/holidays on the Begawan Giri Estate:

www.begawan.com

Jules Haimovitz

Decoration and design by Carolyn M. Lawrence

2700 Neilson Way

Santa Monica

CA 90495

United States

Tel: 001 310 450 0798

Maria Grachvogel

Designs available at her shop:

162 Sloane Street

London SW1X 9BS

Tel: 020 7245 9331

Kristina Borjesson

Apartment design by:

Circus Architects

1 Summers Street

London EC1R 5BD

Tel: 020 7833 1999

Kitchen designers:

FK&F

19 Carnwith Road

London SW6 3HR

Tel: 020 7736 6458

Carlos Miele

Designs available at:

Harvey Nichols

Brompton Road

London SW1X 7RJ

Tel: 020 7235 5000

Browns

26 South Molton Street

London W1K 5RD

Tel: 020 7514 0000

www.carlosmiele.com.br

Joseph Corre and Serena Rees

Agent Provocateur shops
6 Broadwick Street
London W1V 1FH
Tel: 020 7235 0229
16 Pont Street
London SW1X 9EN
Tel: 020 7235 0229
Edra furniture
Enquiries:
Tel: 020 7927 6999

Anna Valentine

Robinson Valentine
4 Hornton Place,
London W8 4LZ
Tel: 020 7937 2900

Karl Edholm

Mect products available through:
twentytwentyone
274 Upper Street
London N1 2AU
Tel: 020 7837 1900
www.mect.se

Stephen Pearce

Shanagarry Pottery
Co. Cork
Ireland
Tel: 00 353 216 46807

Todd Hase

Furniture sold exclusively in the UK at:
Gotham
17 Chepstow Corner
1 Pembridge Villas
London W2 4XE
Tel: 020 7243 0011
Todd Hase, New York:
Tel: 001 212 334 3568
www.toddhase.com

David Champion

Shop:
199 Westbourne Grove
London W11 2SB
Tel: 020 7727 6016
Design company:
Champion Zandberg
Tel: 020 8968 4042

Peter Ting

Painted panels by Brian Kennedy
of Hibernosheen:
Tel: 020 7274 8900

Betsey Johnson

Fashion designs from:
106 Draycott Avenue
London SW3 3 AE
Tel: 020 7591 0005
www.betseyjohnson.com

Wendy Smyth & Richard Gibson

For enquiries about the shop and shirt-making
company:
Tel: 0289 0230388
www.smythandgibson.com

Georgina von Etzdorf

Scarves and fabrics available at:
1-2 Burlington Arcade
Piccadilly
London W1J 0PA
Tel: 020 7409 7789

Tony Baratta

(Fabrics from the Diamond & Baratta range
for Lee Jofa).
For stockists:
Tel: 01202 575457
www.leejofa.com

Anna Zegna

Ermenegildo Zegna
Flagship Store
37-38 New Bond Street
London W1S 2RU
Tel: 020 7518 2700

Alison Kinnaird

For glass-engraving commissions and
details of Alison's Scottish harp courses:
Tel: 01875 830328
email alisonk@templerecords.co.uk

John Rolf

Design and Build
Tel: 01983 873253

Gareth and Miranda Thompson

Design by architects
Adam Caruso and Peter St John:
Caruso St John
1–3 Coate Street
London E2 9AG
Tel: 020 7613 3161
www.carusostjohn.com

Index

Acknowledgements

I would like to thank *The Times* Magazine Editor Gill Morgan for giving me the opportunity to meet and interview so many interesting people and to visit their homes. Also on *The Times* Magazine, Tony Turnbull for bringing it all together each week; Christian Brook and his team for correcting my errors; Graham Ball and his team for inspirational design and layouts; Graham Wood, Lyndsey Price, Isabel Sabine and John Carey on the Picture Desk for their guidance and support. Also to all those who have opened the doors of their homes to me, and to the remarkable team of long-suffering photographers and their assistants who have worked through all manner of conditions, trials and tribulations, as well as good times, to create the wonderful pictures that make these features what they are.

Credits

2 David Loftus; 3 Ray Main/Mainstream; 7 Jan Baldwin/Narratives; 8 left David Loftus; 8 right Ray Main/Mainstream; 12 Jan Baldwin/Narratives; 17 Ray Main/Mainstream; 18–21 Jan Baldwin/Narratives; 22–25 Ray Main/Mainstream; 26–29 David Loftus; 30–33 Ray Main/Mainstream/LTS Architects; 34–37 Jan Baldwin/Narratives; 38–43 Ray Main/Mainstream; 44–47 Paul Massey; 48–57 Jean-François Jussaud; 58–59 Ray Main/Mainstream; 60–61 Ray Main/Mainstream/Artist: Charlotte Valeur; 62–65 Ray Main/Mainstream; 66–69 Jan Baldwin/Narratives/Arch: Circus Architects, Bankside Lofts; 70–73 Graham Wood; 74–87 Ray Main/Mainstream; 88–91 Scott Hawkins; 92–95 David Loftus; 96–99 Jan Baldwin/Narratives; 100–105 Ray Main/Mainstream; 106–109 Jan Baldwin/Narratives; 110–113 Jean-François Jussaud; 114–117 Jan Baldwin/Narratives; 118–133 Ray Main/Mainstream; 134–138 David Loftus; 140–145 Graham Wood; 146–149 Jan Baldwin/Narratives; 150–155 Ray Main/Mainstream; 156–7 Ray Main/Mainstream; 158–163 Eric Morin; 164–167 Tim Clinch/Interior Archive; 169–171 Ray Main/Mainstream; 172–175 Ray Main/Mainstream; 180 Ray Main/Mainstream/Arch: Andrea Zegna; 181 Ray Main/Mainstream/Arch: Luisa Bocchietto; 182–183 Ray Main/Mainstream/Arch: Andrea Zegna; 184–185 Ray Main/Mainstream/ Arch: Luisa Bocchietto; 186–193 Ray Main/Mainstream; 194–199 Tim Clinch/Interior Archive; 200–203 Ray Main/Mainstream.

The author and the publisher would like to thank the following homeowners for allowing us to reproduce the pictures of their homes: Norman Ackroyd; Tony Baratta; Nitish and Monisha Bharadwaj; Kristina Borjesson; Mark Budden; David Champion; Dale Chihuly; Stephanie Churchill; Joseph Corre and Serena Rees; Henry Dent-Brocklehurst; James and Deirdre Dyson; Li Edelkoort; Karl Edholm; Joseph Ettedgui; Graham Fraser and Richard Nott; Bradley and Debbie Gardner; Maria Grachvogel; Jules Haimovitz; Amy and Todd Hase; Wayne and Gerardine Hemingway; Ken Israel; Betsey Johnson; Kenzo; Cath Kidston; Alison Kinnaird and Robin Morton; Mischa Maisky; Carlos Miele; Ann Mollo; Stephen Pearce; Vicky Pepys and Simon Young; Dominic Richards and John Kerr; John Rolf; Wendy Smyth and Richard Gibson; Chantal Thomass; Gareth and Miranda Thompson; Peter Ting; Emanuel Ungaro; Anna Valentine; Georgina von Etzdorf; Anna Zegna

Every effort has been made to trace the copyright holders, architects, designers and owners for this book and we apologise in advance for any unintentional omission. We would be pleased to insert the appropriate acknowledgement in any subsequent editions.